I0834378

Table Of Contents

J.A.M.M with me

A Journey To Your Higher Self

J.A.M.M.S

MINDFULNESS

They Didn't Explain It like this when we were kids

Mindfulness Matters.

By

Shanta Generally, B.Msc

ISBN: 979-8-9854436-4-6

INTRODUCTION

Do you remember the first time you saw a butterfly? Not, just saw it but truly noticed it, the way its wings floated effortlessly, the colors, and design on its wings, and how it shimmered when the sunshine hit it. What about the way it appeared unbothered as it landed on various flowers?

As children, we lived for moments like that without realizing that what we were practicing was mindfulness — the simple art of being fully present. Somewhere along the way, as we grew older, we traded those quiet moments for notifications, deadlines, and distractions.

By now, you've probably heard about how powerful mindfulness can be, how it helps people reconnect with the present moment. Mindfulness is often treated as a "new-age" concept. But the truth is, mindfulness isn't new. It's something we once knew instinctively — before the noise, before the rush, before we forgot how to *just be*. Mindfulness is an ancient practice that has been part of human consciousness for thousands of years. Long before it became a buzzword in wellness circles, mindfulness was a way of living — a natural awareness that many cultures built into their spiritual and daily practices.

In this book, I want to talk about how amazing the practice of mindfulness has been in helping me, as well as others, to live life in the present moment and that it's not something you need to plan for in order to bring this way of being into your life. If you are like me and millions of other humans you may have simply forgotten what it felt like when we were kids sitting quietly observing our surroundings with innocence. When we noticed the birds, butterflies and even the tiniest piece of bird feather floating by, we would pause to observe the beauty, often with curiosity..

They didn't explain it like this when we were kids— the benefits, the meaning, or the importance of simply enjoying being present. Looking back on my childhood it is apparent that life was moving quickly. I used to sit quietly and watch the world unfold — the birds darting across the sky, the shimmer of a butterfly's wings, the way a single feather could dance in the wind. I didn't know it then, but I was practicing mindfulness.

No one taught me to be still or to observe with wonder — it was simply my natural way of being. Somewhere along the way, life became louder, faster, and more demanding. The world taught us to *do* instead of *be.*

This book is a journey back to that stillness — to the quiet wisdom we once knew as children.

"They Didn't Explain It Like This When We Were Kids."

Growing up, we were told to "pay attention," but no one explained *how*. We were told to "calm down," but no one showed us *what that actually meant.* We were expected to focus, behave, and perform — yet mindfulness, the very skill that could have helped us do all of those things with ease, was never part of the lesson.

No one said, "You can train your mind to be still," or "Your breath can bring you peace." Instead, we learned to react, rush, and run toward the next thing. We certainly were not taught to be in the present moment, aware.

But the fact is that, for a long time, I thought *paying attention* meant sitting still — staying quiet — doing as I was told. What I didn't realize back then was that my body could be still while my mind was everywhere else. I could be in a room but not *in* the room. I wasn't really listening, noticing, or connecting with what was happening around me.

We often associate attention challenges with children as "attention deficit," but if we're honest, many adults haven't fully mastered the art of attention either. We scroll through our phones, multitask through our days, and call it productivity — yet our minds wander just as much as theirs do.

Here's the truth: **mindfulness isn't new.** It's ancient — a timeless wisdom that has been waiting patiently for us to remember it.

> "Mindfulness — They didn't explain it like this when we were kids."

That sentence became the title of this book because it's a thought that's stayed with me for years. Why *weren't* we taught this? Why weren't we given the tools to understand our emotions, to sit with our thoughts, or to calm our nervous systems when life felt overwhelming?

We may not have grown up with cell phones or video games, but we still faced anxiety, stress, peer pressure, and uncertainty. The world has changed, but the human experience hasn't.

And that's why mindfulness is just as essential for us as adults as it is for our children. It's not simply about quieting the mind — it's about coming home to ourselves. It's about noticing what's real in this moment, reclaiming our focus, and giving both ourselves and the next generation the gift of presence.

Growing up, I don't remember anyone telling me to pause, to breathe, or to simply notice the world around me. School trained us to chase the next assignment, the next grade, the next goal—but rarely the stillness in between. Yes, we were to sit in class and pay attention, but that just meant looking in the direction of the teacher but not necessarily about being present.

Yet, as a child, I often found myself captivated by things no one else seemed to notice: the quiet rhythm of birdsong at sunrise, the sway of trees bending with the wind, the silver glow of the moon that seemed to follow me home. Those were my secret classrooms, the places where life whispered lessons about peace, presence, and connection. I have to admit, recess was my favorite for a few years, but not just because it meant freedom from the classroom. It was the only time I felt completely alive — the wind brushing against my face, the laughter echoing in the distance, the sound of sneakers hitting the pavement and the squeaking on the gym floor. I didn't know it then, but those were mindful moments. I was fully present, connected to my senses, and completely in the "now," without even trying.

Looking back, those were the moments, the ones that carried wisdom no textbook ever held. And perhaps if we had been encouraged to notice them then, we might have grown up fully understanding mindfulness not as something we must learn later in life, but as something we've always known deep inside.

As most of us grew older, we began to label these moments as "boredom" or "boring" and after all that I have come to understand and know about mindfulness I think to myself " They didn't explain it like this when we were kids".

If you are reading this book, you are probably on a positive path, or a healing or awareness cycle and this book is to be a part of it. I am going to take you on a journey into mindfulness, where we delve into what mindfulness is according to the experts and then I want to share with you the many ways you can add mindfulness into your life today. I have added in a section on mindfulness in relationships and leadership as well in the book, because it is important but let's first discuss the term mindfulness.

The term "mindfulness" refers to the practice of paying attention to our thoughts, feelings, body sensations, and the environment around us in a kind, accepting manner.

Mindfulness also entails acceptance, which is paying attention to our thoughts and feelings without passing judgment on them without, believing that there is a "correct" or "wrong" way to think or feel in any given moment. When we practice mindfulness, our thoughts become focused on what we perceive in the now, rather than on the past or the future.

Its origins can be traced back to Buddhist meditation; nevertheless, a secular practice of mindfulness has recently gained popularity in the world. Thousands of research studies have been conducted to demonstrate the benefits of mindfulness for both physical and mental health. Throughout the book there are several mindfulness exercises added to help to make your reading experience richer overall.

If you are ready to understand what mindfulness is truly about and how you can embrace mindfulness in every part of your life this is the book for you.

“Mindfulness isn’t difficult, we just need to remember to do it.”

- Sharon Salzberg

This book is dedicated to all the beautiful souls who often say out loud "I have ADD or ADHD or squirrel brain"; to the thinkers, dreamers, over-feelers, and over-doers, and the ones whose minds move faster than time itself. You are not broken; you are beautifully wired for curiosity, creativity, and connection.

This book is for you, to remind you that stillness isn't the absence of thought, it's the gentle art of coming home to yourself, one mindful moment at a time. Throughout the book there are activities to help you on your mindfulness journey.

I am open to seeing the truth with clarity and wisdom.

Consider this before we begin:

Why do we expect children to behave like adults,when adults often struggle to model the behavior they expect?

Why do we expect children to behave as adults
when many adults are still learning how to be emotionally mature?

Why do we demand composure from those still growing,
yet forget that growth is a lifelong process for all of us?

These questions are not meant to be answered —
but explored.

Allow them to guide you inward as we begin this journey in mindfulness.

Take a breath.

Sit with these questions before you turn the page.

What Is Mindfulness?

Let's be honest — when most people see the word *mindfulness*, their first thought isn't *exciting*. Some might even think, "boring." But that's not your fault. Your cellphone has already trained your brain to crave constant stimulation — to scroll, swipe, and refresh every few seconds. In fact, research shows our attention shifts about every 47 seconds. Think about that — less than a minute before your mind jumps to the next thing.

Every ping, every notification, every mindless scroll is quietly costing you something; focus, creativity, memory, and even years off your life. How many times today have you picked up your phone without remembering why? How often have you opened an app, only to look up 30 minutes later wondering where the time went?

The truth is, the noise isn't just stealing your time — it's *rewiring your mind.*

But here's the good news: mindfulness is how you take it back.

This isn't going to be another "dry scientific" book filled with endless data and statistics. Instead, it's a guide to *remembering yourself* — to learning how to slow down, reconnect, and truly experience life in real time.

By the time you finish this book, my goal is simple: that your understanding of mindfulness isn't just intellectual — it's *embodied.* You won't just know what mindfulness *means*; you'll know how it *feels.*

Now, this is where I chuckle a tiny bit because I am adding a little more information about a study, but trust me it is informative and a must know. Studies show, the constant scrolling on social media and receiving these notifications frequently increases anxiety, speeds up mental fatigue, and erodes memory. It's actually true. These are things you will care about deeply in ten, twenty or thirty years. This book is not about you sitting cross-legged and chanting. This is an opportunity, a journey into taking back your mind, your focus and your life. If you want to stop living on autopilot and start being fully alive; please continue reading, this is your invitation. And don't worry — you don't have to move to a mountaintop, drink green tea you can't pronounce, or sit cross-legged until your legs fall asleep.

Mindfulness can happen while you're brushing your teeth, waiting in traffic, or trying not to lose your cool when your Wi-Fi freezes during a Zoom call. It's about waking up to *this* moment — even the imperfect, slightly chaotic ones. Mindfulness can show up in the most unexpected places — sometimes it happens in a classroom, when your trainer is enthusiastically explaining the nineteenth PowerPoint slide — and you're focusing on your breath so you don't accidentally roll your eyes or fall asleep. Congratulations, that's mindfulness in action.

When I first heard "mindfulness" I thought there was not much to it, it is about being mind full, let's dive in now and get a little deep. To keep it one hundred, I am still a work in progress and have to think about being mindful on a daily basis.It does not come to me naturally in every awaken moment although I have improved tremendously. I took several courses on mindfulness some years ago and joined a few online communities which collectively have all been helpful. I went on to gain certifications in the area of mindfulness.

Mindfulness is a nonjudgmental awareness of one's reality in the present moment. In this view, mindfulness is a state of being rather than a characteristic. While certain practices or activities, such as meditation, may encourage it, it is not identical to or synonymous with them. Cultivating mindfulness takes time and effort. People are not 'born more aware' than others, and it is not a fixed state.

It requires self-awareness as well as objectivity regarding the benefits we derive from it. Most would say it's simply paying attention, that's it, this is also why I wrote a book and made it part four of the Jamm with me series to help you with understanding on a deep level about this wonderful way of being. I think it's that important that we discuss it in such detail allowing you to become a mindfulness expert and to allow you to help others to shake the misconception that time is in the way preventing them from participating and practicing this renewed exciting modality. Yes, it is considered to be one of our healing modalities centered around awareness. I share in this book mindfulness in a variety of areas in our lives to help make it more beneficial for you as a reader.

Mindfulness is an easy term to remember. It implies that the mind is entirely focused on what is going on, on what you are doing, and the way you are moving through. That may appear insignificant, except the truth is that we frequently lack focus on what is happening in the present moment. Our minds take flight, we lose contact with our bodies, and before we know it, we are absorbed in obsessive thoughts about what just happened or worrying about the future. That makes us nervous and brings on anxiety. Regardless of how far our minds wander, awareness is always there to bring us back to where we are, what we are doing, and how we are feeling. What would you say if I advised you that you have been robbed not of money or possessions but of your attention and the good news is you can gain it back.

Why Is Mindfulness Practice Important?

Mindfulness education is exactly what it sounds like: the intentional integration of mindfulness and mindful meditation ideas, theories, and practices into educational settings and programs.

Mindfulness practice is important because it reconnects you with what's *real* — the present moment. It gives you back the power to respond to life instead of reacting to it. In a world that constantly pulls your attention in a hundred different directions, mindfulness is the pause that brings you home to yourself.

Practicing mindfulness trains your mind the same way exercise strengthens your body. Over time, it helps quiet mental noise, reduce stress, and improve focus. But beyond the science, mindfulness gives you something far more valuable — a deeper sense of peace, clarity, and connection.

When you practice mindfulness, you start to notice the small details that make life meaningful — the warmth of sunlight on your skin, the taste of your morning coffee, and the sound of laughter. It reminds you that joy isn't found in what's next, but in what's *now.*

Mindfulness matters because *you* matter. Your peace matters. And being fully alive — aware, present, and grounded — is one of the greatest gifts you can give yourself. In addition to being a hot topic for scholars and academia, it is relatively simple, affordable, and accessible to anyone at any time.

It may seem crazy to think about teaching mindfulness principles to young children, but it is actually well suited for educational settings—and those situations in which it is most difficult to adopt mindfulness are typically the ones that need it the most! We all have a form of anxiety to some degree and introducing kids to mindfulness can help them to minimize the negative effects of anxiety.

Mindfulness education aims to assist students in learning:

- Self-awareness
- Techniques for calming and focusing the mind based on empathy
- Conscious communication
- Putting mindfulness skills to use in everyday situations.

Mindfulness has been shown in research to have a favorable impact on students in several areas, including:

- Concentration and attention
- Improved grades
- Emotion modulation that is more effective
- Improved school conduct
- Increased sensitivity and flexibility of thought
- Improved social abilities
- Test anxiety has been reduced.

- There is less stress.
- Reduced the frequency and severity of post-traumatic symptoms
- Lower depression rates/severity.

It was not explained to us like this when we were kids. Now that I know the benefits, I am ready to share them with you. We need to ensure kids are aware of all of the benefits and that this information is not only privy to adults, hence the title of the book.

Mindfulness & Your Inner World

The single most important area to practice mindfulness is your inner world: your thoughts, emotions, and energetic state. I really understand this to the core.

What the "Inner World" Really Means

When we say *inner world*, we're talking about the private, often overlooked space where your true experience of life begins. It includes:

1. Your Thoughts

The stories you tell yourself. In book two, I speak heavily on this.
The assumptions you make.
The beliefs you carry from childhood, culture, trauma, or past relationships. We have to challenge these beliefs.
The quiet narratives that shape your confidence, fears, and choices.

2. Your Emotions

The feelings beneath the surface — frustration, hope, sadness, joy, anxiety, shame, gratitude — even the emotions you avoid or suppress.
Your emotional world is asking for attention, not avoidance.

3. Your Nervous System & Body Signals

Your breath patterns, tension, racing heart, sensations, fatigue.
Your body often speaks before your mind does.
This is a huge part of mindfulness we rarely talk about.

4. Your Energy & Boundaries

The weight you carry from others.
The people who drain you vs. those who restore you.
The leaks in your energetic boundaries that leave you exhausted.

5. Your Values & Inner Voice

What actually matters to you — not what the world says should matter.
Your intuition.
Your inner guidance system.
And whether you're aligned with it or abandoning it.

Why We Don't Look Within

In 2019 I had fallen into what felt like depression as I looked closely at my inner world. I felt I was slacking and not living up to my fullest potential. It sucks to have to keep it one-hundred with yourself but it is necessary. It was around this time that I literally grew the most in my life. Most people spend their lives in the outer world because it feels easier to focus on what we *see* rather than what we *feel*. A few reasons:

1. The outer world is louder and more demanding.

- Notifications
- Expectations
- Bills
- Work pressure
- Family pressure
- Social media
- The crisis of the day
- The endless comparison

It's constant noise — and noise keeps us distracted from ourselves.

2. Looking within takes courage.

Self-reflection means you might face:

- Uncomfortable truths
- Unresolved pain
- Patterns that need changing
- Emotions you've been avoiding

Many people were never taught *how* to sit with discomfort, so they avoid it.

3. Society rewards outer success, not inner wellbeing.

We're trained to chase:

- Productivity
- Perfection
- Status
- Approval
- image

Rarely are we taught to prioritize mental alignment, emotional regulation, or energetic protection.

4. Control feels safer than surrender.

We can't control other people, the economy, politics, or how someone treats us.
But we try — and this over-focus on the uncontrollable outer world leads to burnout.

How This Causes Mental Decline

When we disconnect from our inner world, several things begin to happen:

1. Emotional Overload

Unprocessed emotions don't disappear.
They **accumulate**, turning into stress, anxiety, irritability, overthinking, or emotional shutdown.

2. Constant Comparison & Self-Doubt

Living in the outer world means you're always measuring yourself against others. This feeds low self-worth, perfectionism, and chronic insecurity.

3. Mental Fatigue

Trying to control everything outside of you is mentally exhausting.
It leads to rumination, decision fatigue, and feeling mentally "scattered."

4. Nervous System Dysregulation

The body stays in fight, flight, or freeze when the mind is overwhelmed.
This creates:

- Burnout
- sleep issues
- emotional reactivity
- difficulty concentrating
- chronic stress that looks like depression or anxiety

5. Loss of Self

When you focus more on outside validation than inner alignment, you lose sight of:

- what you want
- who you are
- what brings you joy
- what drains your spirit

This disconnection is one of the biggest contributors to the mental health struggles we see today.

Here's why mindfulness is the single most important area to practice when it comes to your inner world.

1. Your inner world directs every outer experience.

Before communication, before decisions, before behavior — everything you do is filtered through your internal state. If you're not mindful of what you're thinking, feeling, or carrying energetically, you're operating on autopilot.

2. Mindfulness of the inner world gives you influence over all other areas.

When you can regulate your thoughts and emotions:

- Your relationships improve
- Your stress responses soften
- Your ability to set boundaries strengthens
- Your creativity expands
- Your career decisions become clearer
- Your wellbeing becomes intentional rather than reactive

It's the root that feeds every branch.

3. Your energy shapes what you attract.

Being aware of what energy you're absorbing or projecting — especially as someone who naturally picks up others' emotions — creates protection, clarity, and freedom from carrying burdens that aren't yours.

4. It is the area you always have access to.

You can't always control your environment, other people, or unexpected life changes. But you can *always* return to your breath, your body, your perspective, and the present moment.

Importance Of Mindfulness In The Workplace

There is a lot of pressure on workers in today's economy, and they are being pushed to accomplish more with less. Well, we now have AI that has been introduced so this may help in a number of powerful ways. Some might argue AI is here to wipe out jobs and today we will not debate. While working longer and longer hours depending on the career path one has selected pressure is mounting. Working in an environment where stress is seen as a badge of honor is unhelpful to the practice of mindfulness. Rushing from one duty to the next can take up so much of our time.

There is a perception of efficiency, but in reality, we're working against the flow of our brains. It's no wonder we're so drained!" Coupled with many of the folks being clickish, and trying to fit in with them is like pulling teeth. Some want to be your friendemy, others your parents, while you are simply trying to take care of your family and find ways to mindfully stay employed. We now know, for sure, that the majority of people who work in corporate environments can work well from the comfort of their homes, but now that most people have returned back into the work force in person, mindfulness is more important than ever and here's a few reasons why.

Social Interactions

1. Noise levels - while many people will be happy to spend time rekindling friendships and creating new friendships, keep in mind that some folks become accustomed to silence during the work day and it may take additional time to adjust. We can all agree it took some years to adjust to the return to office and some are still adapting.

2. Communication etiquette - face to face interactions due to most people wearing masks for so long. We relied on verbal communication and now we are relying on the non-verbal communications again as we understand its importance. Seeing people smiling or seeing people frowning. And now having to feel their energy in person when it is negative sucks. Seeing the facial expressions, mood swings and we have all heard about office politics.

3. Personal space - Remembering to allow individuals to have space and avoid invading their space.

It's really important to be mindful of written communication in the work place. When there is a teachable moment, be sure to use it as such, being mindful not to turn it into a scolding by adding in caps as this can be perceived as yelling. Oftentimes we hear, do not take it personal, but in this section, I want to share with you, take the time to read what you are sending out back to yourself to ensure it cannot be taken as a scolding but rather a helping email allowing growth. I am not lecturing, simply sharing.

There has been a correlation established between the neurobiological benefits of mindfulness and an increase in emotional intelligence, notably empathy and self regulation. We can improve our ability to manage conflict and communicate more effectively as a result of the growth of these areas. As a result, mindfulness allows us to take a step back and explore various views rather than merely reacting to events and making decisions using the least clever part of our brains. Mindfulness assists us in reactivating the rational areas of our brain, allowing us to regain control over our emotions and respond in a more suitable manner when necessary.

The introduction of mindfulness into the workplace does not preclude the occurrence of conflict or the emergence of challenging circumstances. However, when unpleasant situations do arise, they are more likely to be acknowledged, held, and addressed skillfully by the group. It will also certainly keep you from lashing out as you walk away from unwelcomed spaces. With practice, we build the inner resources necessary to negotiate tough, hard, and stressful situations with greater ease, comfort, and grace.

When you become more conscious of your own emotions as they arise, you have a greater range of options for dealing with them. By paying attention to the sensations in your body, mindfulness can assist you in being more conscious of an arising emotion. Afterwards, you can follow these instructions:

- Stop what you're doing right now.
- Take a few deep breaths.
- Become aware of how you are experiencing the emotion in your physical body.
- Consider where the emotion is coming from in your head and how it manifests itself (personal history, insecurity, etc).
- Respond in the most caring and understanding manner possible.

One minute meditation is a simple mindfulness exercise. Find a quiet spot in your office or sit at your desk and slowly breathe, focusing your attention on your breath. Bring your attention back to your breath whenever your mind wanders (which it will). Then take a deep breath and relax as the serenity settles in. Your mind will relax as a result, and you will be able to focus on your workplace tasks. Remembering your purpose for being in the space, you may enjoy the type of work you do, may feel vested in your career and have adult responsibilities, such as bills to pay. This helps you to be mindful of being pulled into nonsense.

Mindful Leadership: The Skill Too Often Overlooked

Mindfulness is talked about everywhere — in wellness spaces, in conversations about mental health, in discussions about self-care — yet when it comes to **leadership**, this skill is often missing from the very people who need it most. Too many leaders are promoted for what they *know* or what they *produce*, not for how they show up, how they treat people, or how emotionally aware they are.

We see this every day in workplaces:
People with impressive titles… who lack human skills.
People with authority… who lack awareness.

People with influence… who lack presence.
People with power… who lack compassion.

And the truth is:
Leadership without mindfulness is just management with blind spots.

Leaders Are Human — But We Forget This

It's easy to look at someone's title and expect perfection, wisdom, and maturity. But leaders are human. They come with insecurities, unhealed wounds, biases, blind spots, fears, and habits formed long before the promotion.This took me some time to truly comprehend. I assumed that they were superheros, with superpowers, LOL I am totally kidding sort of.

The problem arises when leaders *forget* this truth — and when their teams forget it too.
Because when a leader is unaware of their own humanity, they begin to lead from ego, control, and pressure instead of presence, clarity, and connection. I have also witnessed leaders walking by their staff and not acknowledging the employees by simply saying "Good morning" or "Good afternoon" . Some argue that Covid-19 changed the game, but I am not fully convinced.

Promotions Don't Equal Leadership

Many people are promoted because:

- They're excellent at their job
- They know the system
- They're strong individual contributors
- They have seniority
- They're reliable with tasks

But none of these automatically make someone a leader.

Leadership is a skill — not a title. And like any skill, it requires:

- Practice
- Self-reflection
- Emotional intelligence
- Awareness of impact
- Accountability
- Humility
- Willingness to grow

When these qualities are missing, we experience exactly what so many people talk about:
"Bad bosses." "Toxic managers." "Leaders who don't lead."

Some don't know any better. Some know better — but don't put in the effort to grow. And that second group is the most challenging.

What Mindful Leadership Actually Means

Mindfulness in leadership isn't about meditation or being perfectly calm. It's about:

Being aware of your own behavior

How your tone, words, energy, and decisions affect the people around you.

Pausing before reacting

Responding with intention instead of emotional impulsivity.

Creating psychological safety

Making people feel heard, respected, and seen — not judged or dismissed.

Managing your ego

Understanding that leadership is about service, not superiority.

Respecting humanity

Treating people as people, not just as roles or responsibilities.

Being emotionally present

Actually listening, actually noticing, actually caring.

Owning your impact

If your behavior hurts, confuses, or overwhelms your team, you address it — not avoid it. I often wonder if some get into positions just for the pay.

Why Mindfulness Makes You a Better Leader?

Mindful leadership builds trust — not fear.
It increases respect — not resentment.
It strengthens teams — it doesn't fracture them.

When a leader is mindful, people feel:

- Safe to speak
- Safe to make mistakes
- Safe to grow
- Safe to ask questions
- Safe to think creatively
- Safe to be human

This is where real leadership happens.
This is where teams thrive.
This is where people feel inspired rather than intimidated.

A Message to Leaders (and Aspiring Leaders)

If you are leading a team, a project, or even one person — your mindfulness matters.

You don't have to be perfect.
You don't have to have all the answers.
You don't have to know everything.

But you *do* have to know yourself.

Because leadership begins with inner work.
The more mindful you are, the more aligned your leadership becomes.

A mindful leader leads with:

- Awareness
- Empathy
- Courage
- Self-regulation
- Authenticity
- Emotional intelligence
- Accountability

These are the qualities that turn a title into a calling.

Reflection Questions for Leaders

1. What energy do I bring into the room when I lead?
2. Do people feel safe expressing concerns around me?
3. Do I lead from ego, fear, or presence?
4. What emotional triggers impact the way I lead?
5. Am I willing to grow or do I expect others to grow while I stay the same?
6. What would my team say it feels like to work with me?

Mindful Communication as a Leader

Communication is the heartbeat of leadership. You can have strategy, vision, expertise, and authority — but if you cannot communicate with awareness, empathy, clarity, and intention, your leadership will always fall short.

Mindful communication is not about speaking softly or being overly cautious. It's about being *conscious* of how your words, tone, decisions, and presence influence the people you lead.

Leadership communication has power.
It can build or break trust.
It can inspire or intimidate.
It can create connection or disconnect.
It can empower or shut people down.

Mindful leaders choose the first path.

What Mindful Communication Really Means

Mindful communication is rooted in presence. It means being fully aware in the moment, not distracted, not reactive, and not leading from assumptions or ego.

A mindful leader communicates with:

Clarity

Say what you mean — without confusion, mixed signals, or hidden expectations.

Compassion

Speak in a way that respects the person, even when addressing tough situations.

Curiosity

Instead of assuming, a mindful leader asks questions to understand.

Awareness of Tone

Your words matter, but your tone often speaks louder.

Active Listening

True listening is not waiting for your turn to speak — it's being fully present for what's being said *and* what's being felt.

Intentional Pausing

A pause prevents emotional reactions from becoming permanent decisions.

The Impact of Unmindful Communication

We've all experienced one or more of these:

- Leaders who talk "at" people, not with them
- Leaders who interrupt or dismiss
- Leaders who communicate from frustration
- Leaders who avoid difficult conversations
- Leaders who use fear instead of clarity
- Leaders who give vague directions, then blame the team
- Leaders who expect mind-reading

Unmindful communication creates:

- Resentment
- Confusion
- Low morale
- High turnover
- Stress and anxiety
- Walls between leaders and their teams

And the worst part? Many leaders don't even realize the damage they're causing because no one feels safe enough to tell them.

The Pillars of Mindful Communication

Speak with Purpose, Not Pressure

Before speaking, pause and ask:

- What is the intention behind my words?
- Am I reacting or responding?
- Will this message uplift, clarify, or empower?

Mindful communication is not rushed — it's intentional.

Listen to Understand, Not Defend

Most communication problems happen because people "hear" words but ignore emotions.

Mindful leaders listen for:

- Meaning
- Feelings
- Unspoken concerns
- Patterns
- Needs

Listening is leadership.
Silence is a skill.
Presence is powerful

Use Tone to Build Safety

Your tone sends a message your words cannot wipe away.

Ask yourself:

- Does my tone invite conversation or shut it down?
- Does it feel safe for people to be honest with me?
- Do I talk *with* people or *down to* them?

Mindfulness requires emotional self-awareness, especially in stressful moments.

Communicate Expectations Clearly

Many leaders assume their team "should already know." But clarity eliminates confusion.

A mindful leader:

- Gives clear directions
- Sets clear timelines
- Defines expectations
- Follows up with transparency
- Checks for understanding without being condescending

Clarity is kindness.

Don't Avoid Hard Conversations — Elevate Them

Mindfulness is not avoidance.
It's presence.

Difficult conversations become easier when approached with:

- Compassion
- Respect
- Honesty
- Emotional steadiness
- A willingness to understand the other person's perspective

Avoidance leads to chaos.
Mindfulness leads to growth.

Respond, Don't React

Reactivity is emotional autopilot.
Mindful communication requires consciousness.

A mindful leader uses:

- Breath
- Awareness
- Self-regulation
- Timeouts if needed
- Reflection before speaking

Responding builds trust.
Reacting burns bridges.

Close Conversations with Understanding

Mindful communication doesn't end abruptly. You ensure:

- Both parties understand the next steps
- Feelings and concerns have been acknowledged
- Nothing important is left unspoken

This creates a clean emotional and professional closure.

A Mindful Leader's Communication Checklist

- Am I present at this moment?
- Do I know my intention before speaking?
- Am I listening without judgment?
- Is my tone respectful and steady?
- Have I asked clarifying questions instead of assuming?
- Have I communicated expectations clearly?
- Am I responding consciously, not reacting emotionally?
- Did I acknowledge the other person's feelings and experience?
- Are we leaving the conversation with shared understanding?

Closing Reflection

Mindful communication is not about perfection — it's about awareness.
It is a leadership superpower that transforms how you lead, how people follow, and the emotional health of your team.

When you communicate mindfully, you don't just lead with authority —
you lead with humanity.
And that is the kind of leadership people remember, respect, and willingly follow.

Mindful Communication as a Leader Exercise Section:

Use this page to reflect deeply on the way you communicate, the energy you bring into leadership spaces, and the areas where growth is calling you.
This is your moment to pause, assess, and realign.

Self-Reflection Check-In

1. How would I describe my communication style in leadership moments?

(Consider tone, clarity, listening habits, and emotional presence.)

✎ *Write your reflection:*

2. When I'm under stress, how does my communication shift?

Do I react quickly? Shut down? Speak sharply? Over-explain? Avoid conversations?

✎ *Write your reflection:*

---

3. What is one communication habit I know I need to improve?

(Think honestly — this is where growth begins.)

✎ *Write your reflection:*

Awareness Building: My Leadership Impact

4. How might my communication style impact the people I lead?

Consider morale, trust, confidence, creativity, and psychological safety.

✎ *Write your reflection:*

---

5. What feedback have I received (directly or indirectly) about my communication?

This could be words people said, body language you observed, or patterns you've noticed.

✎ *Write your reflection:*

____

____

____

6. What emotions do I bring into conversations when I feel unheard, challenged, or misunderstood?

Awareness here is key for mindful leadership.

✎ *Write your reflection:*

____

____

____

Growth & Intention Setting

7. What does mindful communication look like *for me* as a leader?

Define it in your own words:
(Is it calm tone, clarity, pausing before responding, active listening, emotional control, compassion?)

✎ *Write your reflection:*

____

____

8. What is one mindful communication habit I commit to improving this week?

Choose a small, consistent action.

Examples:

- "I will pause before responding."
- "I will ask clarifying questions instead of assuming."
- "I will listen without interrupting."
- "I will reflect on my tone before I speak."

✎ *Write your intention:*

____

____

____

9. What support, tools, or systems can help me communicate more mindfully?

(Journaling, breathwork, accountability partner, leadership training, therapy, coaching, etc.)

✎ *Write your reflection:*

____

____

____

Affirmation for Mindful Leaders

"I lead with presence, clarity, and compassion.
My communication reflects my growth, my awareness, and my commitment to becoming a better leader."

Leadership, communication, and daily interactions all begin in the same place — within you. The way you show up in the world is directly influenced by the state of your mind, your breath, and your internal rhythm.

Mindfulness isn't just something you *think* about; it's something you *embody*.
It's a lived practice, a moment-to-moment awareness that grows stronger the more you nurture it.

Up until now, we've explored mindfulness as a mindset — how it shapes your leadership, your communication, and the energy you bring into relationships and conversations.

But mindfulness is not sustained by intention alone.
It deepens through practice.
Through stillness.
Through presence.
Through reconnecting with your body in a world that constantly pulls you out of it.

This is where meditation becomes essential.

Mindfulness meditation gives you a space to return to yourself — to regulate your nervous system, quiet the noise, release tension, and build the emotional resilience needed to lead, love, and live with clarity.

And one of the most accessible, grounding, and transformative practices is the Body Scan Meditation.

The body scan teaches you how to listen inwardly.
It shows you where you're holding stress, where you've gone numb, where you need compassion, and where your body is asking for rest or rebalancing.

It is a bridge between your awareness and your physical experience — a gentle way to return home to yourself.

In the next section, we will explore mindfulness meditation practices beginning with the body scan what it is, why it works, and how you can use it to cultivate a deeper presence in every area of your life.

Types Of Mindfulness Meditation Practice

The distinction between mindfulness and meditation is one of the most frequently misunderstood concepts. Mindfulness meditation is a practice in which you intentionally and consciously devote time to cultivating mindfulness.

Conscious awareness with mindful attitudes is mindfulness. A single breath or your entire life can be a time period for which you can cultivate a state of mindfulness. This skill can be honed while standing in line, conversing with a loved one, or simply strolling along the street.

Common mindfulness meditations/practices;

- **Body scan meditation**: This is usually done lying down, but you can do it in any position that seems comfortable to you. Become aware of your bodily sensations in a mindful manner, one sensation at a time, as you progress through this meditation. Furthermore, you will begin to notice how easily your attention is drawn away from one thought to another, and you will learn to be nice to yourself rather than self-critical when this occurs.

- **Movement meditation**: Yoga, Tai Chi, Qi gong, or some other physical mind-body activity is commonly used for movement meditation. This style of meditation is focusing on your bodily sensations, breathing, and actively watching and possibly letting go of any thoughts or emotions that occur as you practice. Slow walking meditation is another option that is occasionally utilized.

- **Breathing space meditation**: This is a three-minute meditation. Do this a few times a day and whenever you are in a high-stress situation or experiencing a difficult emotion. Instead of avoiding your experience, the goal is to cultivate a careful awareness of it. This method has been scientifically proven to be far more efficient than avoidance. Later in the book you will find mindful breathing techniques.

- **Expanding awareness Meditation**: is commonly referred to as sitting meditation, but it can be conducted in any position. The meditation entails focusing on your breath, body, sounds, thoughts, and feelings, often in that sequence, and then cultivating an open awareness in which you are choicelessly aware of whatever is most prevalent in your consciousness. In book two of the Jamm with me series, meditation is covered extensively.

You can break down the expanding awareness meditation into separate meditations, each powerful and transformative in themselves:

1. Mindfulness of breath meditation: it entails paying attention to the sensations of your in-breath and out-breath.

Bring your attention back to the present moment whenever your mind wanders.

2. Mindfulness of body meditation: it entails paying attention to the physical sensations in your body from moment to moment. You can also practice this in conjunction with breathing awareness.

3. Meditation on sound mindfulness: Being aware of sounds as they arise and pass away. If there are no ambient sounds, you can simply listen to the quiet and see what effect it has on you.

4. Mindfulness of thought meditation: Thoughtfulness is important, being aware of your thoughts as they arise and flow through your mind, as well as having a sense of distance between yourself and your thoughts. You don't judge or attach to your thoughts, allowing them to come and go as they please.

5. Mindfulness of feelings Meditation: it entails observing whatever emotions come in you. You pay attention to where you feel the emotion in your body and give your feelings a quality of acceptance and curiosity.

6. Open awareness meditation: also known as choiceless awareness meditation.Because you become aware of whatever is most prevalent in your consciousness without selecting. Any of the aforementioned meditation experiences are all easy to practice.

Mindfulness meditations can be divided into two categories: visuals and contemplation. In these meditations, mindfulness is defined as paying attention to the here and now, rather than focusing on the past or the future. People who have a preference for visual meditations find them useful.

The two main visual meditations are:

1. Mountain meditation: This meditation assists you in cultivating stability and groundedness, as well as a sense of centering yourself.

2. Lake Meditation: This meditation focuses on the beauty of accepting and allowing experiences to be precisely as they are.

Adding in grounding exercises can be helpful and fun because they bring you back into your body and out of your busy mind. So often, our thoughts are racing ahead — worrying about the future or replaying the past — and grounding helps anchor us in the *now.* When you engage your senses through touch, sight, sound, taste, or smell, your nervous system receives the message: *I'm safe.*

This simple shift can lower stress, slow your heart rate, and create a calm awareness that feels both peaceful and empowering. And the best part? Many grounding practices — like walking barefoot on grass, feeling the texture of an object, or taking a few mindful breaths — are surprisingly enjoyable. Now that you understand why grounding is so beneficial, let's take a moment to actually experience it.

Understanding mindfulness is only half the journey — the other half is practice. Grounding is one of the most accessible ways to bring your awareness back home to yourself, especially when your mind starts to drift.

How Mindfulness Elevates Leadership Styles

Mindfulness is not a leadership style on its own — it is a strengthener. It enhances the way you show up, the way you communicate, and the way you lead people, regardless of your natural approach. Some leadership styles benefit from mindfulness more immediately, while others are transformed by it over time.

Leadership Styles That Benefit Most from Mindfulness

1. Autocratic Leaders

Mindfulness softens harshness, reduces reactive behavior, and helps these leaders communicate with clarity instead of control.

2. Transformational Leaders

Mindfulness grounds their big vision, keeping them present and connected instead of overly idealistic or scattered.

3. Charismatic Leaders

Mindfulness helps them stay authentic, balanced, and aware of their impact — preventing ego-driven leadership.

4. Coaching & Servant Leaders

Mindfulness enhances empathy, deep listening, and emotional intelligence — their core strengths.

5. Situational Leaders

Mindfulness sharpens self-awareness, making it easier to read people and adapt with intention instead of guesswork.

How Mindfulness Strengthens All Leadership Styles

- Improves communication — you pause before speaking, creating clarity and calm.
- Increases emotional intelligence — you recognize your own triggers and others' needs.
- Supports better decision-making — you respond with intention instead of reacting from stress.
- Enhances presence — your team feels seen, heard, and valued.
- Builds psychological safety — people feel comfortable bringing ideas and concerns forward.
- Reduces burnout — mindful leaders regulate their energy and model healthy behavior.

Mindfulness turns leadership into a human-centered practice instead of a task-driven role.

How to Identify Your Dominant Leadership Style

Ask yourself:

1. What do people consistently say about your leadership?

(Feedback reveals patterns.)

2. How do you naturally show up during challenges?

Do you take charge? Ask for input? Inspire? Coach?

3. What energizes you most when leading?

Motivating? Teaching? Organizing? Visioning? Delegating?

4. What approach do you default to under stress?

This often reveals your true style: directive, collaborative, hands-off, or nurturing.

5. Which style feels the most authentic to your personality?

Leadership works best when it aligns with who you are, not who you think you "should" be.

Reflecting on these questions will reveal the style that naturally guides your leadership actions.

How to Blend Leadership Styles Mindfully

Blending styles makes you adaptable, emotionally intelligent, and effective in diverse situations.

Here's how mindfulness helps you blend styles with purpose:

1. Pause and assess the situation.

Every scenario calls for something different — vision, structure, empathy, or collaboration.

2. Consider the people you're leading.

Mindfulness helps you read energy, needs, and readiness levels.

3. Choose the style that supports the goal, not your ego.

Sometimes you need to inspire. Sometimes you need to guide. Sometimes you need to step back.

4. Stay flexible.

Mindfulness keeps you aware of when to shift, soften, or strengthen your approach.

5. Reflect after leading.

What worked? What didn't? How did people respond? Mindful reflection helps you refine the blend over time.

Elevate Leadership

Mindfulness doesn't change who you are as a leader — it elevates you.
It brings clarity to your strengths, softness to your edges, and adaptability to your leadership toolkit.

With mindfulness, you don't just lead with authority — you lead with awareness, intention, and humanity.

Grounding Technique

In this next section, you'll find a short grounding exercise. Think of it as a reset — a way to clear your energy, calm your mind, and reconnect with the present moment before continuing on.

Grounding Technique: 5-4-3-2-1

Name 5 things you can see:

1.

2.

3.

4.

5.

Name 4 things you can touch

1.

2

3.

4.

Name 3 things you can hear

1.

2.

3.

Name 2 things you can smell

1.

2.

Name 1 thing you can taste

1.

A beautiful mind is like a canvas of colors — mindfulness is the brush that brings its brilliance to life.

Concepts for Entering Through Doors

One thing that excites me about writing this book is providing concepts and exercises that I use frequently as a part of my mindfulness practice. Pause for a moment and think about the fact that you enter and exit doors daily. When you wake up each morning you walk into your bathroom or out of your bedroom, your front door, back door, or garage door.

Entering a door can symbolize the start of something new — The start of a new day, a class, a meeting, a moment of mindfulness, or a chapter in life. Every time you step through a doorway, you have the opportunity to *leave what came before behind* and fully engage with the present moment.

For example, as I walk into a client's home preparing for a sound therapy session, taking a deep breath before the session begins, signaling, *"I am here now."*

Doors mark transitions between spaces, tasks, or mental states. Being aware of crossing thresholds can help you consciously move from one role or mindset to another.

Pause for a breath before entering a new space — notice how your body feels, what your mind is holding onto, and set an intention for what you want to bring through the doorway.

Choice and Opportunity

Entering through a door can represent choice: you decide what you allow into your life, your mind, and your energy. Notice what you carry with you into each new space, are you bringing stress, distractions, or peace and focus?

Week one mindful exercise

When you are entering through doors, notice the height of the door(s) , notice the hardware on the door, is the door made of glass, wood, iron.

Notice how you feel entering into the room as you are noticing the surroundings.

Notice how you feel when leaving out spaces where you walk through the door.

When you think of doors what thoughts come to mind now that you have completed this exercise?

____

____

Over the next five days each time you walk into a new door observe the door(s) pause for a moment to think of how you feel, just simply notice. If you would like to journal about your experience here is space below for you to do so.

____

____

Journal Art

Tap into your creativity

Below Draw a door using your non-dominate hand

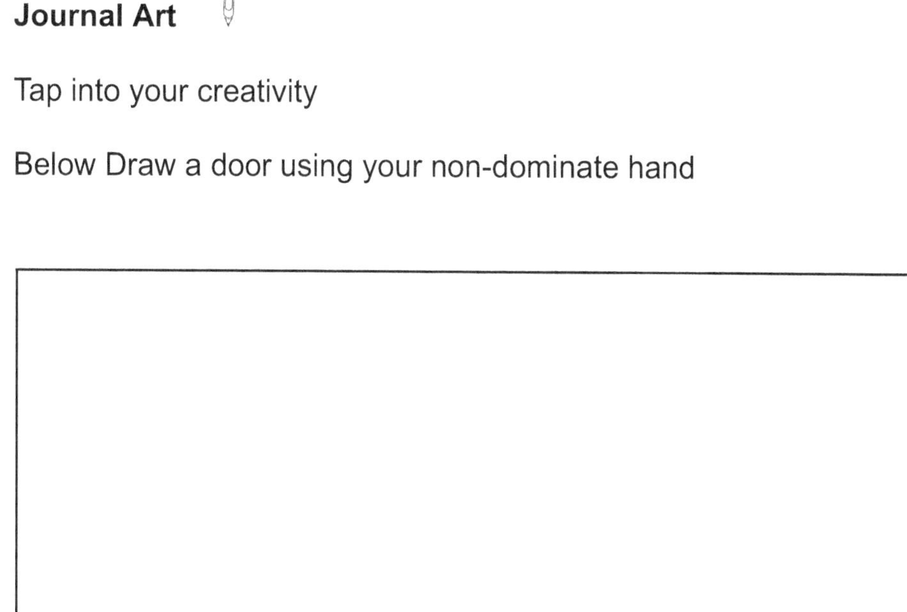

"The present moment is the only moment available to us, and it is the doorway to all moments." - ***Thich Nhat Hanh***

Doors can represent new opportunities

Journal 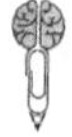

What is it that gets in the way of you practicing mindfulness?

Have you ever turned off your cell phone to relax?

Can you commit to an electronic detox for 24 hours?

Do you have any fears that you have not dealt with?

What negative thoughts do you have on a daily basis?

Do you believe you have control over your thoughts?

Establishing a Daily Routine.

Take Back Control Through Awareness.

Start your day off with mindfulness. One of the exercises that I do daily is observe my initial thoughts when I awake in the mornings. I want to expand on it a bit in this book. Observing my thoughts has been helpful in identifying negative thoughts and being able to pinpoint what the thoughts were that were causing the negative thoughts and bringing on that yucky feeling, if I was having negative thoughts. How often does the alarm go off and you roll over to hit the snooze button and think "ugh " as soon as the thought of work goes through your mind. Or have you awakened in the middle of the night happy you have three hours remaining before it's time to get up and prepare for work. I can think of plenty of things over the years I have been able to learn about myself by simply witnessing my thoughts. One was that if I allowed myself to, I could have lazy tendencies. It is rare that I actually feel like doing deep cleaning, heavy organizing or decluttering my closet. Once I get started I am okay but my thoughts do not often lead me there without me having to think of the benefits of taking action. The goal is to become more mindful about everything we do in life. It is critical that the message is understood.

1.) Mindful to observe your first thoughts in the morning

2.) Mindful to observe your thoughts throughout the day

Be mindful to not spend much time on focusing on negativity due to the mental and emotional effects.

Mental and Emotional Effects of Negativity

Constantly focusing on negative thoughts can fuel worry, hopelessness, and despair. Your brain gets trained to default to negativity making it harder to notice positivity and it triggers your body's stress response, releasing cortisol and adrenaline. This keeps your nervous system on high alert, even when there's no immediate danger. If you have ever been in the presence of anyone who often thinks negatively, you may have observed the impact on their mood and motivation. I personally do not enjoy being in the company of those who think negatively frequently. It becomes uncomfortable to not challenge their way of thinking by offering a new view point.

Cognitive Distortions
You may start developing thinking patterns like catastrophizing, black-and-white thinking, or assuming the worst.

Reduced Emotional Resilience
It becomes harder to bounce back from challenges when your mindset is stuck in a negative loop.

Negativity Bias Intensifies
The more you focus on the negative, the more your brain will notice and hold onto it — it becomes your default filter.

Physical Effects

Chronic Stress Response
Negativity activates the sympathetic nervous system (fight or flight), increasing cortisol and adrenaline.

Weakened Immune System
Ongoing stress and negativity can suppress immune function, making you more prone to illness.

Sleep Disruptions
Overthinking or replaying negative scenarios can make it hard to fall or stay asleep.

Fatigue & Tension
The body often mirrors the mind — negativity can lead to chronic muscle tension and exhaustion.

Behavioral Effects

Isolation or Withdrawal
Constant negativity can strain relationships, leading to loneliness or feelings of being misunderstood.

Procrastination & Self-Sabotage
Negative thinking often leads to inaction or a fear of failure.

Reduced Motivation
You may lose interest in things you once enjoyed or feel like "what's the point?"

Spiritual Effects

Disconnection from Purpose
It becomes harder to feel aligned, inspired, or connected to your "why" when you're focused on what's wrong.

Lack of Gratitude or Wonder
Negativity can block the ability to experience awe, appreciation, or spiritual peace.

Energetic Imbalance
It may leave you feeling heavy, blocked, or out of sync with your intuition or higher self.

The Good News:

The brain has neuroplasticity, meaning you can rewire it. Practices like:

- Gratitude journaling
- Mindful breathing
- Reframing thoughts
- Spending time in nature
- Engaging in uplifting conversations
- Practicing self-compassion
- Positive Visualization

- Learning something new

Mindfulness helps break this cycle. By observing negative thoughts without judgment, you stop feeding them with energy. Instead of getting pulled into a spiral of worry, mindfulness teaches you to notice, label, and *release* the thought, creating space for clarity, calm, and more balanced thinking.

Characteristics Of A Mindful Person

NON-JUDGMENTAL OBSERVATION

Practicing mindfulness entails being able to pay attention to your own experience without becoming preoccupied with assigning judgment to any of it. Developing an attitude of having an active and curious interest in things exactly as they are, without making any attempts to change or reject any of it, is the goal of this practice. When one is not afraid of what may happen in their experience, nor is one unsettled by the unexpected, there is no need to dread.

People, events, thoughts, feelings, and sensations are all observed in their whole. This balanced observation leads to an improved understanding of impermanence, complexities, and complexity.. The judgments of "good" and "bad" are put aside in favor of open-minded, curious observation. There is no need to reject things that are unpleasant. This is a skill that I had to study in order to fully implement this into my life and is constantly evolving.

ACCEPTANCE

Observing ourselves with nonjudgmental curiosity is extremely challenging when we are unwilling to accept all of our characteristics in their whole. When we are experiencing unpleasant or difficult thoughts, feelings, or sensations, we can practice taking an active stance of acceptance toward them by noticing them and exercising an active stance of acceptance toward them. Being attentive requires accepting that we will not always experience pleasant states of being, which is necessary in order to develop more mindfulness.

When we practice mindfulness, it allows us to sit with difficult thoughts and feelings with a greater sense of calm... less fear and resistance. No matter what we are experiencing internally, awareness requires us to take an actively accepting position toward it. As a result of our internal state, we have no sense of pride or guilt — it is simply acceptance of everything that "is." This is where real awareness and growth lives.

IMPARTIAL WATCHFULNESS

Mindfulness does not take sides or become fixated on the "need" to interpret circumstances in a particular manner in every given setting. As a result of mindfulness, which involves not becoming overly "connected" to the need for particular points of view, we are more able to see reality as it truly is. When we approach problems with an open mind, we have a better chance of coming up with answers and ideas that are innovative and actually in our best interests. We have a wider wealth of potential directions at our disposal when we examine reality in this open and unbiased manner, as opposed to when we become fixated on a specific direction that the ego has determined is "ideal."

Consider how difficult it is, on a general basis, to remain objective when discussing our own personal experiences. When contemplating the condition of a friend or coworker, it is frequently significantly more difficult to maintain an "objective" perspective. When it becomes all about "us," objectivity is frequently thrown to the wind and forgotten. It is possible to become more in tune with the internal watching self that we all possess via the practice of mindfulness. It enables us to see our own ideas, feelings, and personal difficulties with the same clarity and openness that we might be able to experience for someone else.

NON-CONCEPTUAL AWARENESS

Another English term for mindfulness is “bare attention.” There is no thinking or interaction with cognitive processes in the way that the majority of us are accustomed to seeing or experiencing them. Mindfulness is merely the act of looking and observing. Although it is aware of thoughts and memories, it does not become entangled in them or feel the need to classify or categorize them. This state of pure consciousness is devoid of assigning meaning and combining with thoughts and feelings — it is the state of pure awareness.

We have the opportunity to experience what it feels like to watch everything as if it were the first time when we practice mindfulness. It enables us to look at both the familiar and the unfamiliar with a new set of eyes, amazement, and interest, as if for the first time. It is not "attempting" to see anything or failing to see anything at all. Because it has no goal, it is not concerned with what it "needs" to observe or not notice in order to function properly. Try to imagine what it would be like to be able to detangle yourself from your deeply ingrained patterns of thinking and emotion in this manner. What might you see that you have not even considered looking at before?

PRESENT-MOMENT AWARENESS

Mindfulness is anchored in the present moment... in this very moment. This pure awareness exists only in the present moment, when you are aware of your breath, the sensations in your body, and your experience as you read the words on this page. It does not exist elsewhere. We have the potential to reconnect with the present moment in a completely different way when we practice mindful awareness.

Many people in our fast-paced culture experience a sense of "automatic pilot," and making the decision to become more present in our life is a good way to snap out of that state. Meditation, rather than allowing oneself to be trapped in a mental dream of the past or future, is a method for bringing oneself back to the present moment – back to one's reality.

Choose a memory from your past to reflect on in order to demonstrate the difference between present-moment conscious awareness and being mentally or emotionally distant/removed from the present moment. Consider the characteristics of that period of your life... how you were feeling, thinking, and experiencing things. Can you imagine it in your mind's eye? Now... become conscious of the fact that you are recalling it. This awakening is taking place in the current moment. Engaging in present-moment awareness entails being able to observe your thoughts as they occur in the present moment.

NON-EGOTISTIC ALERTNESS

For the time being, take a look around the room and / or your surroundings. What are you seeing? Recognize how you feel on the inside. What's going through your mind, body, and soul? You may be looking at the world and yourself through the prism of your own self-perception. It's perfectly normal. We've discovered how the world and its inhabitants interact with us. After all, it was by making demands that we learned to get our needs satisfied as infants and children. We discovered who was beneficial and who was detrimental by how they treated us.

In order to cultivate mindfulness, you must adopt a new perspective on the world and your own experiences in it. Allowing yourself to let go of your egotistical self-drama is the first step. It involves paying attention to things as they are, not as they are viewed from your perspective. Suppose for a moment that you're experiencing discomfort in your leg. In the past, you could have said, "I'm in pain." You can learn to perceive sensations without attaching yourself to them through mindfulness.

Nothing needs to be emphasized or highlighted. When something is upsetting "you," there is no need to make it more dramatic. With mindfulness, instead of "my pain," you simply notice "pain." Not to diminish or ignore your sorrow, but rather to look at it in a new light. When you begin to pay attention to your experience more fully with nonegotistic awareness, you'll realize that you're less prone to respond to it.

AWARENESS OF CHANGE

Because even while mindful awareness focuses solely on the present moment (which is all that exists), it is able to recognize that change is inevitable. Mindfulness is the ability to observe the natural flow of experience and all life in the here and now.

As you become more aware of your own thoughts, feelings, and experiences, this can be extremely helpful. Your internal experience will no longer need to be a part of your identity if you realize that it is fleeting. It's possible that you're feeling elated, depressed, furious, nervous, guilty, or afraid right now. It doesn’t matter how strong or short-lived an emotion is.

When we practice mindfulness, we become more conscious of the ways in which our thoughts and feelings can alter our perception of the world around us, as if we were wearing a pair of rose-colored glasses. As we become more aware of the effect our own mood has on the moods of those around us, our reactivity and resistance decreases. For example, we can become more sensitively aware of our own experiences and how we affect others as a result of this enhanced awareness.

PARTICIPATORY OBSERVATION

There is a common misconception that mindfulness is a type of passive observation... It is not a passive process. To be more specific, mindfulness needs the meditator to behave as both a participant and an observer at the same time in a setting instead of just watching. You become a part of the group, event or activity. In this sense, you might be both the observer of your experience and the experience itself at the same moment. As naturally as thoughts, feelings, and sensations develop, they do so within the same vessel that is observing the occurrences.

At the same time that you are watching your feelings arise within you, you are experiencing them. Mindfulness does not imply a rejection of your current state of affairs or a retreat into nothing but dispassionate observation. It is a sort of open observation in which the observer is having an experience of what it is witnessing. In spite of the fact that mindfulness is objective, it is neither cold or unfeeling. Awakening to life is a conscious engagement in the continuing process of being alive."

This involves immersing yourself, interacting, taking notes and reflecting. The benefits can be a richer, more authentic insight and capturing nuances that otherwise could be missed through surveys or interviews. It also helps to understand unspoken norms, values or feelings. Learning by doing and blends the experience with documenting. This is often used when studying cultures,or communities.

Benefits Of Mindfulness

Let's be honest, the word "benefits" can sound a little dry. But here's the thing: the benefits of mindfulness aren't just nice ideas on a page — they are *life-changing*, and I've experienced this personally.

I wanted mindfulness in my day-to-day life because I needed tools to manage stress, stay grounded, and show up fully for my family, my work, and myself. What I discovered surprised me: the simple practice of being present didn't just make tough moments easier, it enhanced the joy in ordinary ones, too. Yes, I love my journaling, affirmations, meditation and mindfulness aka J.A.M.M (S) . We will get into the "S" in J.A.M.M.S in the last book of this five part series.

Mindfulness gives you access to clarity, calm, focus, and resilience — the kind of benefits that make daily life feel less like a scramble and more like something you can navigate with intention. And here's the exciting part: these benefits aren't reserved for a certain age or stage of life. They're accessible to everyone, and knowing them can inspire you to keep showing up for your practice — even on the chaotic days.

So as we explore the benefits, I invite you to notice which ones speak to you most. Which ones make you think, *"Yes, I want more of that in my life"?* Because that is exactly where motivation and lasting change begin.

Mindfulness was identified as an effective mental health practice in a large-scale analysis of more than 400 prior studies, and it was found to be beneficial for almost all people in terms of improving their physical and psychological well-being.

1. Decreased Depression

One of the most significant benefits of mindfulness is a reduction in depression. It can help alleviate the symptoms of depression and may even help prevent the recurrence of similar symptoms in the future if taken regularly.

2. Improved Emotional Regulation

It is also possible that practicing mindfulness will assist you in better understanding and managing your emotions. It is the ability to exert control over one's own emotions that is referred to as emotional regulation. This entails being able to both amplify and suppress emotions based on the scenario and the need for control. This talent can play a significant influence in one's mental well-being as well as the ability to manage one's emotions.

The emotional regulation benefits of mindfulness can make it easier to cope with your feelings, which can eventually enhance many aspects of your life, such as your relationships and overall well-being, as well as your overall health.

3. Reduced Anxiety and stress

Chronic stress is a significant problem for many adults, and it has been shown to be associated with a variety of health problems, including an increased risk of developing depression and anxiety.

When it comes to relieving anxiety and stress, mindfulness can be extremely beneficial.

4. Better Memory

Mindfulness may also have the ability to improve your memory in certain situations. Those of us who have forgotten an important meeting or misplaced our vehicle keys are well aware that even simple, everyday memory issues can be a huge inconvenience. Proactive interference is a type of memory interference that occurs when older memories interfere with your ability to access newer ones. This is the cause of many of these moments of forgetfulness.

5. Improvements in Cognitive Function

Mindfulness does more than only help you concentrate on your thoughts and remember things more easily; data suggests that it may also contribute to your capacity to think flexibly and coherently in certain situations. It stands to reason that practicing mindfulness can have an impact on your way of thinking. After all, the practice itself is all about becoming more aware of your own thoughts without passing judgment on what you're thinking or feeling. Sustained attention, cognitive flexibility, and the ability to suppress your thoughts and attention in spite of the distractions around you are all important cognitive abilities in mindfulness,(cognitive inhibition).

These cognitive abilities are required for a wide range of everyday activities. They provide you the ability to think rapidly and adapt to changing circumstances. This type of ability also allows you to go from one job to another with ease, making it easier to concentrate on activities and solve difficulties more effectively.

6. Stronger Relationships

Practicing mindfulness may also have a beneficial effect on your interpersonal interactions, according to recent research. I discovered in one of my studies that persons who were more cognizant of their own flaws and imperfections were also more accepting of their partner's flaws and defects.

People who are more accepting of their spouses report higher levels of satisfaction in their relationships as a result. Instead of concentrating on their partner's imperfections and attempting to rectify them, mindfulness helps people accept the fact that their mate is not always flawless.

7. Mindfulness Promotes Physical health

Mindfulness can also be beneficial in alleviating the symptoms of a variety of different medical illnesses. Mindfulness activities have been associated with reductions in lower back pain, rheumatoid arthritis, psoriasis, Type 2 diabetes, and fibromyalgia, among many other conditions.

People who are struggling with chronic illness may find mindfulness to be beneficial since it can help them improve their mood and reduce their stress levels.

8. improves well-being.

Increasing your capacity for mindfulness helps you develop a variety of attitudes that are conducive to living a happy life. Being attentive makes it simpler to relish the pleasures of life as they occur, assists you in being completely engaged in activities, and provides you with a higher ability to cope with stressful situations. Many people who practice mindfulness report that they are less likely to become preoccupied with worries about the future or regrets about the past, are less preoccupied with concerns about success and self-esteem, and are better able to form deep connections with others as a result of focusing on the present moment.

9. Reduce Rumination

It has been demonstrated in several studies that mindfulness helps to minimize rumination. People in a 10-day intensive mindfulness retreat, for example, reported considerably higher awareness and a decrease in negative affect when compared to participants who did not participate in the mindfulness retreat. In addition, they reported fewer depressed symptoms and less ruminating than the other group.

Principles Of Mindfulness

Over the years, in my roles as a coach, facilitator, podcaster, mother, and wife, I've realized something: even when we *think* we understand mindfulness, practicing it fully in the chaos of daily life is another story. Between deadlines, family demands, endless notifications, and the noise of our own minds, it's easy to lose track of what it really means to be present.

That's why I want to pause here and offer the core principles of mindfulness — not as abstract ideas or rules to follow, but as practical guides to help you *live* mindfulness in every moment. These principles aren't just for meditation cushions or quiet mornings; they're tools for real life — for the messy, beautiful, unpredictable life you're living right now.

Before we dive into each principle, I want you to take a breath and notice this: understanding mindfulness intellectually is one thing — experiencing it is where the real transformation happens. And that's exactly what these principles are here to support.

1. Non-judging.

As we begin to practice mindfulness, we become more conscious of our mental patterns, how preoccupied our brains genuinely are, and the narrative that we are constantly running — one that is constantly criticizing our experiences — and we are able to change them.

Keep track of how many times you categorize your experiences as nice (and want to hold on to them), terrible (and want to throw them away), or neutral as you begin to tune into your mind (not interested in it). It is possible to acquire mindfulness by taking on the role of an objective observer of one's own experience.

Consider the following scenario: you'll find that your mind has wandered early on in your practice. If you find yourself unable to pay attention to your breath, instead of berating yourself, simply acknowledge that your mind has wandered, relax back into your body (without making any judgments), and restore your focus to your breath with an attitude of kindness and compassion for yourself.

Our understanding of ourselves and our experiences is growing as a result of mindfulness practice, and we are learning to see things as they are rather than as we would like them to be.

2. Patience

An idea that things will only emerge in their own time characterizes this perspective. The truth is that cultivating awareness takes time; there are no shortcuts to this process.

When you recognize that you are not being aware and that your mind is wandering, it is really beneficial to be patient with yourself and allow yourself to catch up. It takes time and effort to develop new habits and neural pathways in your brain, and it is only through repetition, repetition, and more repetition that these new neural pathways become hardwired.

Remember that mindfulness is a practice of forgetting and remembering, so be gentle with yourself. When you notice your attention drifting away from the exercise and bring it back, remember that you are reinforcing your new habit of waking up to the present moment by noticing and returning to it.

3. Beginner's mind

It is the formation of a mindset that is willing to observe everything as if it were the first time that is referred to as "beginner's mind." Just consider how young toddlers are at the moment and how this makes us feel like we are experiencing the world through their eyes as well.

We're sort of resetting our experience and bringing the mindset of someone who has never had any experience before to any encounter that we're having as a method of getting ourselves off of autopilot and paying attention to what we're doing.

Can you walk into your next meeting as though it is the first time you have seen your colleagues and been in that meeting room?

OR, could you go through your front door as if it were the first time you had seen your partner and children?

What impact may this have on your attention, the way you relate to your experience, and the way you interact with the people in your life if you did it?

4. Trust

Trust can be demonstrated in various ways, one of which is trust in the practice of mindfulness. A significant amount of scientific research has been conducted to demonstrate the benefits of mindfulness training. What would be the consequences of trusting what we are learning and the practices we are putting into practice? What exactly would we be letting go of if we did this?

Second, through practicing mindfulness, we are learning to pay more and more attention to our inner knowledge as well as to our own inner wisdom. We are gaining greater objectivity and confidence in the validity of our own thoughts, feelings, and intuition as we go through life together. We're learning to put our faith in ourselves.

5. Non-aggressive (non-striving)

We spend so much of our life attempting to attain a goal that we are rarely actually present for the journey we are on; rather, we are assessing where we are in relation to the objective and determining whether or not this is good or bad in terms of an ideal future state.

By placing our faith in the practice we are engaging in and maintaining a patient attitude, it is possible that we will become more content with where we are right now. A willingness to accept the moment as it is, and to accept ourselves as we are, is what it takes to be present. We are not attempting to get anywhere or solve problems; rather, we are paying attention to the awareness of the actuality of our experience as it is.

6. Acceptance

In learning to accept our existing circumstances, we are teaching ourselves to accept things for what they are without attempting to change them or wishing for them to be otherwise.

The fact that this is neither a passive response or a resignation does not imply that it is. It is true that we are more aware of our experiences and how we are responding to them; we are more cognizant of how we are responding.

This is a basic transformation in our attitude toward the difficult, resulting in a fundamental shift in our relationship with the things in our lives that give us suffering and sorrow. When we don't fight against them, we aren't causing ourselves any pain or suffering.

7. Learning to let go

This is a way of letting things be as they are, of accepting things for what they are as they are. We allow them to be, and in doing so, we allow them to depart.

Consider how often you may find yourself holding onto things during difficult situations and the effect this has on our minds; we frequently become very distracted, reactive, and rigid in our thinking as a result.

Take a step back and observe what we are experiencing without passing judgment on it. This is the first step in letting go. As a result of doing so, we have the experience that it will come to pass.

8. Gratitude

Participants in mindfulness programs frequently mention that they have learned to be more appreciative of their lives as a result of the practice.

Yet, as a result of our tendency to operate on autopilot, we frequently take for granted the miracle of life — the fact that we are breathing and that our body is operating properly at the present moment.

As soon as we express thanks for this current moment and acknowledge that we have a wonderful body and that we are still here, our experience shifts. This attitude serves as a gentle reminder to us of this.

9. Generosity

When we honestly devote our time and attention to others, we are able to experience a greater sense of interconnectedness.

It has been demonstrated again and again in studies that prioritizing someone else's needs over your own, and giving what will make them happy, has a high correlation with psychological health and well-being.

Mindfulness Exercise

Reading about mindfulness is helpful, but real transformation happens when you *practice it*. That's why I included this section of mindful exercises — a place for you to do more than just read. These exercises are meant to be *experienced*, written about, carried with you, and even shared with others. I have added exercises throughout the book, I wanted to share those with you early in the book.

Think of it as an old-school reference guide for your modern life — a tangible toolkit for grounding, focus, and presence.

You can use these exercises anywhere: at home, on a break at work, during travel, or even as a mindful pause while waiting in line. They are not meant to be perfect or complicated — just simple, practical ways to bring mindfulness into your everyday moments.

My hope is that this becomes more than a book on a shelf. I want it to be something you open, engage with, and even gift to someone else — a small, portable reminder that mindfulness isn't a concept; it's a practice you can hold in your hands and carry in your heart.

There are many different mindfulness activities indicated below that were explicitly designed with the goal of reducing social anxiety disorder in mind; however, the first three exercises are often used in group sessions to enhance awareness and are therefore included here.

1. The Raisin Exercise

This is an excellent introductory exercise for beginners to start practicing mindfulness because it can be done by anyone with any type of food and can be done anywhere (although one with an interesting or unusual texture, smell, or taste is best).

In this exercise, the facilitator hands out a handful of raisins to participants and instructs them to imagine they have never seen a raisin in their lives before. The facilitator then instructs students to pay close attention to the following aspects of the raisin: how it appears; how it feels; how their skin responds to its manipulation; its scent; and its taste (if applicable).

By concentrating on a single object, such as the raisin, the participant's mind is expected to be brought back to the present, to what is immediately in front of them. We may be accustomed to raisins, but we may not be familiar with taking the time to recognize them.

By focusing on the raisin in their palm and making it a point to observe everything about it, people are less likely to be investing energy, time, and attention on worrying or ruminating about other aspects of their lives.

When you follow these directions and pay attention to what is going on around you, it becomes much simpler to concentrate on the task at hand. If your thoughts do wander, it is perfectly normal. Bring it back to the activity in a gentle manner.

2. The Body Scan

Used by many in the mindfulness space during meditations, coaching sessions and I also use this during some of my sound bath sessions. The Body Scan is a popular mindfulness exercise among those who practice mindfulness. In fact, I have added the body scan in a few areas within the book for you to understand the best ways to use it. You can use this as an instructor or for your personal use guiding yourself through the scan. Props and instruments are not required, and it is also simply accessible to the majority of novices who are interested in learning. Let's walk through each step as if you are guiding participants through the body scan.

Step 1

The Body Scan begins with the participants lying on their backs with their palms facing up and their feet falling slightly apart. This exercise can also be done sitting on a comfortable chair with feet resting on the floor;

Step 2

lie down very still for the duration of the exercise, and move with awareness if it becomes necessary to adjust their position;

Step 3

participants begin by bringing awareness to the breath, noticing the rhythm, the experience of breathing in and expelling out. The facilitator explains that nobody should try to change the way they are breathing but rather just hold gentle awareness on the breath;

Step 4

how it feels, the texture of clothing against the skin, the contours of the surface on which the body is resting, the temperature of the body and the environment;

Step 5

bring your awareness to the parts of the body that are tingling, sore, or feeling particularly heavy or light, s/he asks the participants to note any areas of their body where they don't feel any sensations at all or are hypersensitive.

Body Scans are performed by running over each portion of the body, paying close attention to the sensations felt in each place. The scan is normally performed in a methodical manner, beginning at the feet and progressing upwards as follows:

Start at the toes;

The rest of the feet (top, bottom, ankle);

Lower legs;

Knees;

Thighs;

Pelvic region (buttocks, tailbone, pelvic bone, genitals);

Abdomen;

Chest;

Lower back;

Upper back (back ribs & shoulder blades);

Hands (fingers, palms, backs, wrists);

Arms (lower, elbows, upper);

Neck;

Face and head (jaw, mouth, nose, cheeks, ears, eyes, forehead, scalp, back top of the head);

When the Body Scan is finished and the participants are ready to return to the room, they can slowly open their eyes and move to a comfortable sitting position naturally. The body scan is one of my favorite mindful exercises.

3. Mindful Seeing

For some people, the lack of visual stimulation might be oppressive. After all, not everyone is born with a good imagination.

Anyone who identifies with this may find the activity of Mindful Seeing beneficial.

It's a simple activity that only requires a window with a view. The facilitator leads the group through the following steps:

Step 1

Find a space at a window where there are sights to be seen outside;

Step 2

Look at everything there is to see. Avoid labeling and categorizing what you see outside the window; instead of thinking “bird” or “stop sign,” try to notice the colors, the patterns, or the textures;

Step 3

Pay attention to the movement of the grass or leaves in the breeze. Notice the many different shapes present in this small segment of the world you can see. Try to see the world outside the window from the perspective of someone unfamiliar with these sights;

Step 4

Be observant, but not critical. Be aware, but not fixated;

Step 5

If you become distracted, gently pull your mind away from those thoughts and notice a color or shape again to put you back in the right frame of mind.

4. Mindful Listening

Mindful listening is a vital skill to have, and it may be a fun group mindfulness activity to practice. Human beings thrive when they feel completely "heard" and "seen," and careful listening allows us to take a break from concentrating on ourselves or our own responses.

It is possible to generate an inner stillness in which both parties feel free of assumptions or judgment, and the listener is not distracted by inner chatter while acquiring vital positive communication skills through this method of listening.

The Mindful Listening exercise involves these steps, you can do this with family and friends:

Step 1: invite participants to think of one thing they are stressed about and one thing they look forward to;

Step 2: once everyone is finished, each participant takes their turn in sharing their story with the group;

Step 3: encourage each participant to direct attention to how it feels to speak, how it feels to talk about something stressful as well as how it feels to share something positive;

Step 4: participants are instructed to observe their own thoughts, feelings, and body sensations both when talking and when listening;

Step 5: after each participant has shared, you can break into small groups and answer the questions below. Next, regroup and have a discussion and debrief with the following questions.

Those questions are:

How did you feel when speaking during the exercise?

How did you feel when listening during the exercise?

Did you notice any mind-wandering?

If so, what was the distraction?

What helped you to bring your attention back to the present?

Did your mind judge while listening to others?

If so, how did "judging" feel in the body?

Were there times where you felt empathy?

If so, how did this feel in the body?

How did your body feel right before speaking?

How did your body feel right after speaking?

What are you feeling right now?

What would happen if you practiced mindful listening with each person that you spoke with?

Do you think mindful listening would change the way you interact and relate with others?

How would it feel if you set the intention to pay attention with curiosity, kindness, and acceptance to everything you said and everything you listened to?

"Mindfulness is the aware, balanced acceptance of the present experience. It isn't more complicated than that."

- **Sylvia Boorstein**

Mindfulness Exercise For Daily Living

1. Wake up Early

Making the decision to wake up a bit earlier in the morning not only helps you to begin your day with awareness, but it also allows you to have more time to enjoy life itself.

Give it a shot for a week or so and see how it goes. Even a few more minutes in the morning can make a significant difference in how much more enjoyable your mornings are.

2. Awaken with Gratitude

The practice of beginning each day with thankfulness helps us teach our thoughts to search for the good things in life rather than dwelling on the difficulties, frustrations, and slights we have met throughout the previous weeks.

While the number of things you are grateful for and the length of time you spend in gratitude are important factors in making this habit effective, it is the intensity of your focus and feelings surrounding the effort that is most important to its effectiveness.

It is important to immerse yourself in the emotion of thankfulness so that you feel deeply and genuinely blessed throughout a mindful gratitude practice.

3. Practice a Morning Breathing Exercise

Do you pay close attention to how you're breathing right now? The practice of thoughtful, focused breathing, even for 10 minutes a day, can help you relax and reduce your stress levels.

A drop in heart rate and relaxation of the muscles are caused by slow, deep, rhythmic breathing, which stimulates the parasympathetic nervous system as a result of the reflex stimulus.

4. Notice Your Thoughts

The first thing that happens when you allow negative thoughts to run wild in the morning is that you miss out on the most productive and creative time of the day. Because the loop of rumination and negative thinking begins as soon as their feet touch the ground, many people experience anxiety and dread when they first wake up.

Once you've been aware of your poor habit, you may begin to modify it by developing a new habit that is as simple as observing. Your ideas lose some of their power over you when you separate yourself from them and merely observe them with detachment.

5. Practice Shower Meditation

Showering is already a part of most people's morning ritual, whether they realize it or not. However, by including a little meditation session in this routine, you can devote more time to practicing deep thinking and generating happy thoughts for the rest of the day.

Sure, shower meditation might sound hokey, but look at it this way: You know how you get some of your best ideas while you're in the shower? Well, the same principle applies here. Warm water has a relaxing impact on the mind, allowing it to operate on autopilot, allowing it to generate inspiring ideas.

Shower meditation is one of the best mindfulness exercises since it doesn't ask you to do anything new; all you have to do is do the same things in a different way.

To act in a more careful and deliberate manner.

6. Drink Water

Drinking water is a habit that is similar to the mindfulness exercise described above. It is nothing revolutionary; it is simply a matter of taking the time to perform a common good habit in a more thoughtful manner.

It is extremely beneficial to drink a glass of water first thing in the morning for a variety of health reasons. After going for seven to eight hours without drinking anything, your body requires water to rehydrate—especially if you plan to follow up your water with a cup of caffeinated coffee or tea to help you feel more awake.

In addition, drinking a large glass of cool water immediately after waking up increases your metabolism by 24 percent over the next 90 minutes. It also has the additional benefit of improving mental and physical performance throughout the day. As a result of being dehydrated, you may suffer feelings of fatigue and exhaustion, as well as headaches and mood swings.

7. Read Inspirational Content

Choose to read uplifting, inspiring, and motivational books or articles instead of starting your day with information overload (such as checking your email or turning on the television).

Developing your own beliefs and assumptions, as well as reading and considering other people's thoughts and viewpoints, is a crucial aspect of becoming a mindful person and stretching yourself in the process. This necessitates making a conscious decision to read books that elevate and educate you, as well as novels that support your values, aspirations, and interests.

8. Set a Daily Intention

Think about the difference between the following two statements:

A. I plan to complete my project by 3:00 p.m. today.

B. I intend to complete my project by 3:00 p.m. this afternoon.

Which of the following statements is more powerful? With one of these statements do you feel the most confident that the person making the remark will follow through with it?

It comes as no surprise that intending to do something has more power than planning not to do something. Intention denotes a sense of determination, will, and perseverance. An intention possesses a confidence that a plan will never be able to match.

When you set a daily objective, you are committing to seeing it through to completion, come hell or high water. You are resolved to give top priority to this action or mindset at the expense of other activities in order to ensure that it is completed successfully.

A sense of purpose, as well as the inspiration and desire to attain your goals, are all provided by intentional actions.

9. Be Present with Your Family

How many families, how many households around the world start their days with little to no interaction with the ones they care about the most?

What are we striving for, if not to spend quality time with our loved ones?

A family's mindfulness behaviors must be taught and modeled by at least one adult member. You may be a role model for your husband and children when it comes to the value of mindfulness, especially in your relationships.

The best way to begin is by demonstrating the power of being present, even if only for a few minutes before starting your work or school day.

10. Connect with Nature

For most people, the only time they spend outside is during the short walk from their house to their car on a busy morning. Although it may just take a few minutes out of your morning routine to spend time outside, it can have a significant impact on your mental and physical health.

Spending time in nature can help to enhance your immune system, alleviate symptoms of sadness and anxiety, improve attention and creativity, reduce stress, and improve your memory.

11. Do a Sun Salutation Yoga Routine

Yoga, like meditation, is a practice that may be divided into many different styles, each with its own set of exercises, philosophies, and desired objectives. The majority of practices include physical postures (asanas) that are intended to cleanse the body while also providing physical strength and stamina.

Yoga works with the energy in the body, through pranayama or energy-control, as well as breath-control, in order to calm the mind and reach higher states of awareness. Pranayama is the control of one's own energy in the body.

12. Recite Positive Affirmations

Using positive sentences to describe who and how you want to be in the present tense, as if your desired outcome has already occurred, affirmations can be used as a mindfulness habit to help you relax and be more present in your life. Good affirmation habits can be established first thing in the morning, and they can have a positive impact on the rest of your day.

Intentionally and frequently practicing positive affirmations can strengthen chemical pathways in the brain, strengthening connections between two neurons and thus increasing the likelihood that the same message will be transmitted again in the future. In book two of the Jamm with me series the topic of affirmations is discussed extensively.

13. Practice Mindful Driving

If your morning routine includes driving to work, conducting errands, or dropping off your children at school, you are well aware of how "mindless" individuals can be in morning rush-hour traffic and how unpleasant driving in a car may be on a regular basis.

If you are aware that driving causes you to experience feelings of wrath, stress, and anxiety, you can alter your perspective on this task by engaging in mindfulness practices.

Take a few deep breaths as soon as you get into your vehicle.

While driving, avoid turning on the radio or engaging in other distracting activities. Put your phone on vibrate or quiet mode.

As you begin to drive, make a conscious effort to pay attention to your surrounding environment.

You can simply identify your feelings if you are stuck in traffic or someone cuts you off. If you are frustrated or angry because someone has cut you off, notice your feelings and simply identify them.

Take advantage of traffic jams or other unavoidable stops to practice taking a few deep, relaxing breaths.

Once you've reached your location and turned off the engine, take three deep breaths, focusing on releasing the exhalation, and then relax for a while to collect your thoughts.

14. Practice Transition Breathing

In the past, how many times have you dashed from your car into your workplace or office and instantly begun doing something—checking emails, chatting with coworkers, or diving into a project—without pausing to think?

Of course, getting to work immediately appears to be a productive and diligent move, but a part of you is lagging behind, still processing the thoughts or sensations you brought into the office with you.

Breathing exercises might assist you in controlling and quieting your thoughts. Prior to switching gears, take a few deep breaths and center yourself so that you can approach your work with greater serenity and focus afterwards.

15. Clear Your Desk

Visual clutter is both distracting and upsetting to the observer. It causes you to become more inefficient and less productive. It interferes with your ability to think creatively and clearly. Moreover, it conveys the message to others in your immediate vicinity that you are chaotic and scattered.

Taking time to clear and organize your desk allows you to practice focused mindfulness for a few minutes as you select where to place your belongings, what to keep, and what to toss away.

Once your desk is free of clutter, you have created an environment conducive to more mental and emotional energy and attention as you begin your work. I enjoy having a few items on my desk that help to make the space feel as if it is a stress free zone in the event I am having any type of struggle that day.

16. Practice a Mindful Email Check-In

The act of checking our email on our phones or computers is one of the more addicting actions that we engage in. The majority of us will check our inboxes dozens of times a day, and this is a habit that causes significant stress and anxiety in our lives.

In addition to making you more productive and focused, breaking this poor habit and becoming more attentive about how you approach your email inbox will allow you to be more conscious and less reactive to the unpredictable rewards of email. When speaking with others about simple things such as email management, you may be surprised to find that others may have tips that can help you to manage your email inbox in ways that can eliminate email anxiety. One of my goals is to improve this area in my life.

17. Group Your "Things to Do" List

Did you know that your mind prefers to organize by clustering little, related objects together into cohesive holes rather than by categorizing them?

Grouping related chores, such as doing all of your writing in one sitting or completing all of your housekeeping tasks in one sitting, increases your productivity and focus. You'll also be forced to work for a longer period of time in order to achieve a "flow state," in which your task becomes simpler and more mindful.

Batching jobs that are similar in nature and need similar resources will aid in streamlining their execution while also reducing stress and procrastination.

18. Practice the Pomodoro Technique

Using the Pomodoro Technique, work periods are divided into 25-minute intervals (known as Pomodoros), with a 5-minute rest in between each interval.

The goal of this method is to boost productivity. By concentrating intensively on a job for a short amount of time, you can increase your mental agility (and efficiency). After that, you should take a little pause to replenish your batteries.

Despite the fact that strong concentration in any work appears to be tough, concentration in any endeavor is undoubtedly a mindfulness practice. It provides the opportunity for you to become fully immersed in your task with sufficient engagement that you achieve the flow state that we discussed previously.

For individuals who have problems concentrating, the Pomodoro Technique will undoubtedly assist you in remaining present with your task while not becoming fatigued or succumbing to distractions quickly.

The Pomodoro Technique is comprised of five fundamental steps:

1. Determine the task that needs to be completed.

2. Start by setting a timer for twenty-five minutes.

3. Continue working on the task until the timer goes off. Record the Pomodoro in writing as a task that has been completed.

4. Take a short break from work (5 minutes).

5. Complete four Pomodoros and then take a longer break (15–20 minutes).

19. Practice "Slow Work"

Slowing down with whatever you do is a vital component of being present in the moment and achieving a sense of flow with your work. The sense of success that comes with completing tasks quickly and efficiently is lost when you hurry from one task to the next, trying to cram in as much effort as possible.

Investing extra time in each task and doing it thoroughly will ultimately result in increased productivity and success.

Consider slowing down your activities rather than rushing through them in order to complete everything on your to-do list—whether it's washing the dishes or finishing a job project.

These are what I consider to be enjoyable mindfulness activities. This is because you are taking mundane tasks and turning them into something pleasurable, rather than just another block to cross off the list as "complete."

20. Be Present with Peers

When it comes to their professions, one of the most common grievances people have is the way they deal with their bosses, clients, or colleagues. Performance expectations combined with personality differences create a climate that is ripe for conflict and rivalry to flourish.

Civility, kindness, and compassion are frequently regarded as being incompatible with many workplace situations in which "the bottom line" takes precedence over effective communication and collaboration.

By being more present with the individuals you work with, you may contribute to a more emotionally intelligent workplace as well as to your personal sense of well-being. Even a few minutes every day spent being more present can make a significant difference in your level of job satisfaction.

21. Create Mindful Meetings

Most of us enjoy mindful meetings where the facilitator has an agenda, a purpose for the meeting, simply put, the intent is clear.

Do you work in an atmosphere where you are required to attend meetings on a regular basis? If this is the case, you are surely aware that meetings can be a significant drain on your energy and efficiency. Despite this, some meetings are essential for your role or for your voluntary activities in general. In addition to participating in meetings called by others, you may be responsible for facilitating meetings on your own initiative.

To make meetings more meaningful for you and the other attendees, you can practice mindfulness before and during meetings, rather than thinking of them as a waste of time or energy.

A list of five tactics you can use to get the most out of each meeting you attend is provided below for your consideration:

. Arrive with clear intentions. Before the encounter, pay attention to your feelings. Ask yourself what you want to take away and what value do you want to bring.

. Prepare one or two strategic questions. Questions can shift the entire quality of the meeting. Keeping the mindset of a beginner can help in this area as when we are new to something we often prepare and take notes.

. Be an active listener. It is okay to listen attentively and speak less. Mutual respect.

. Speak with purpose. Tie your point to the meeting goals if possible. Keep feedback concise. Provide constructive criticism.

. Maintain your concentration and leave with clear next steps. Confirm deadlines and if necessary how progress will be tracked.

Mindful Eating

Mindfulness eating was introduced to me as an adult although I have to admit, my mother would often say "slow down" reminding my brother, Craig and I to chew our food. Advice we did not take. I found I ate less and enjoyed the taste of the food much more as an adult once I slowed down to actually chew and taste the food. It was difficult at first, especially when I was eating something that tasted good. I wanted to eat fast and chew less out of habit. I often would say in a joking manner that I didn't chew the food, I swallowed it. I often overeat when I am hungry. I have found when the space between meals is further apart, implementing this practice can be challenging but upon thinking of "mindfulness" you automatically slow down to break the food down properly before swallowing.

Mindful eating is defined as the practice of keeping an in-the-moment awareness of the food and drink that you consume. It entails paying attention to how food makes you feel, as well as the signals your body sends regarding flavor, enjoyment, and fullness after eating it. Practicing mindful eating encourages you to just acknowledge and accept rather than criticize your own sentiments and ideas, as well as your own physiological sensations. Purchase, preparation, and serving your meal are all aspects of the process, as is the act of enjoying your food.

Mealtimes are typically rushed occurrences for many of us due to our hectic daily schedules. We find ourselves eating in the car on the way to work, at the desk in front of a computer screen, or parked on the couch in front of the television while watching. When we eat, we do so blindly, cramming food down our throats regardless of whether or not we are still hungry. As a matter of fact, we eat for reasons other than hunger, such as to satisfy emotional demands or to reduce stress, as well as to cope with negative emotions such as grief, anxiety, loneliness, or boredom. Conscious eating is the polar opposite of this type of unhealthful "mindless" consumption. This can also cause excessive weight gains for children and adults as eating becomes a form of entertainment.

To practice mindful eating, you don't have to be flawless, or eat only the proper foods all of the time, or never eat on the move again. In mindfulness eating there are no strict rules for how many calories you can consume or which foods you must include or avoid in your diet. The focus here is more so about focusing all of your senses and being fully present while you shop for, prepare, serve, and consume your meal (and drink) this will lead you to healthier choices eventually when implementing your mindful practice.

While mindfulness isn't for everyone, many individuals have discovered that by eating in this manner, even for a few meals a week, they may become more in tune with their bodies and their emotions. Avoiding overeating, making it easier to change your dietary habits for the better, and taking pleasure in the improved well-being that comes with eating a healthier diet are all benefits of doing so.

I have met a few people who had various surgeries to assist with weight loss and during the early stages after their procedures practicing mindful eating appeared to be at the top of the list with every meal. Upon them removing mindful eating, many found themselves right back where they were prior to having the procedures. In addition to mindful eating, there may need to work on a mindset centered around eating. This is something many overlook but it may be necessary if eating has unofficially become a form of entertainment, it could sound like this " I am not hungry, I am full but feeling restless or needing something to do" Let's talk about the benefits of mindful eating.

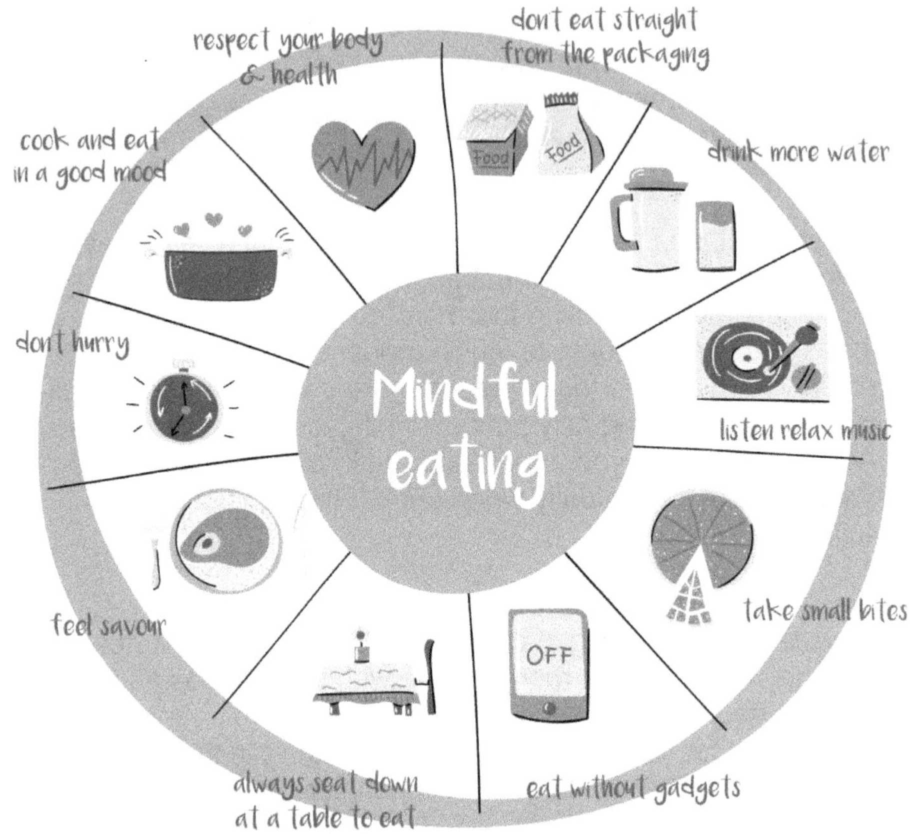

Benefits Of Mindful Eating

The ability to savor both your food and the experience of eating comes from paying close attention to how you feel when you eat—the texture and flavors of each mouthful, the hunger or fullness signals your body sends to your brain, and how different foods affect your energy and mood—as you eat. Being conscious of the food you consume can help you digest your food more efficiently, feel fuller with less food, and make better eating choices in the future. It can also assist you in breaking free from bad eating and food-related habits.

Eating thoughtfully can assist you in the following ways:

Slow down and take a break from the hustle and bustle of your day, which will help to relieve tension and stress.

Take stock of and make changes in your relationship with food—for example, by helping you become more aware of when you turn to food for reasons other than hunger.

As you learn to slow down and savor your meals and snacks more completely, you will derive greater pleasure from the food you eat in general.

Make better meal choices by paying attention to how each type of food makes you feel after you've consumed them.

Eating more slowly can help you digest your food better.

Eat less food and feel filled sooner by eating less.

Make a stronger relationship with your food by learning more about where it comes from, how it is produced, and the journey it has made to reach your plate.

Consume food in a more nutritious and well-balanced manner.

How to practice mindful eating

To cultivate mindfulness, you must engage in a task while maintaining complete awareness of your surroundings. Practicing mindful eating is paying full attention to your food rather than eating on "automatic pilot" or while reading, looking at your phone, watching TV, daydreaming, or planning what you're going to do later in the day. When your focus wanders away from your food and the experience of preparing, serving, and eating it, gently bring it back to it.

At start, try practicing mindful eating for short periods of time (five minutes or less), and then gradually increase your time commitment. And keep in mind that you can start practicing mindful eating as soon as you make your grocery list or look over the menu at a restaurant. Take the time to carefully consider each item you add to your list or select from the menu.

- Start by taking a few deep breaths and considering the health value of each different piece of food. While nutrition experts continually debate exactly which foods are "healthy" and which are not, the best rule of thumb is to eat food that is as close as possible to the way nature made it.

- Employ all your senses while you're shopping, cooking, serving, and eating your food. How do different foods look, smell, and feel as you chop? How do they sound as they're being cooked? How do they taste as you eat?

- Be curious and make observations about yourself, as well as the food you're about to eat. Notice how you're sitting, sit with good posture but remain relaxed. Acknowledge your surroundings but learn to tune them out. Focusing on what's going on around you can distract you from the process of eating and take away from the mindfulness experience.

- Tune into your hunger. How hungry are you? You want to come to the table when you're hungry, but not ravenous after skipping meals. Know what your intentions are in eating this specific meal. Are you eating because you're actually hungry or is it that you're bored, need a distraction, or think it's what you should be doing?

- With the food in front of you, take a moment to appreciate it—and any people you're sharing the meal with—before eating. Pay attention to the textures, shapes, colors and smells of the food. What reactions do you have to the food, and how do the smells make you feel?

- Take a bite, and notice how it feels in your mouth. How would you describe the texture now? Try to identify all the ingredients, all the different flavors. Chew thoroughly and notice how you chew and what that feels like.

- Focus on how your experience shifts moment to moment. Do you feel yourself getting full? Are you satisfied? Take your time, stay present and don't rush the experience.

- Put your utensils down between bites. Take time to consider how you feel—hungry, satiated—before picking up your utensils again. Listen to your stomach, not your plate. Know when you're full and stop eating.

- Give gratitude and reflect on where this food came from, the plants or animals involved, and all the people it took to transport the food and bring it onto your plate. Being more mindful about the origins of our food can help us all make wiser and more sustainable choices.

- Continue to eat slowly as you talk with your dining companions, paying close attention to your body's signals of fullness. If eating alone, try to stay present to the experience of consuming the food.

Remember, Mindful eating is not about rules, restriction, or perfection.

It is about returning to the simple truth that your body deserves to be nourished with presence, respect, and awareness.

"Mindful eating is a way to become reacquainted with the guidance of our internal nutritionist."

— Jan Chozen Bays, M.D.

Eating locally grown foods that are in season is best when possible. Shopping at the local farmers market is a plus.

Mindful Walking

I have to admit, this is one practice that I think about on a daily basis. If I am not walking, I think to myself I should walk and focus on the act of walking or as I am walking I am reminded to implement the practice of mindful walking. A mindful stroll is a great method to rid your thoughts of clutter and regain your sense of focus after a stressful day. It also serves as an excellent excuse to get out into the fresh air. Several studies have demonstrated that taking a pause to look at or be in nature can have a rejuvenating effect on the brain, allowing you to free up your thoughts when you are feeling stuck and increasing your levels of concentration.

Take five to ten minutes a day to incorporate mindful walking into your daily routine by engaging all of your senses, sight, hearing, smell,taste and touch are all important to bring awareness to your body and surrounding environment.

Here's how to do it:

As you walk, notice how your body feels.

Pay attention to how your legs, feet and arms feel with each step you take.

Feel the contact of your foot as it touches the ground, and the movement of your body as you move into your next step.

If you become lost in thought as you continue to walk, use the next step as an opportunity to start over.

Now using your sense of sight, look around and try to notice every detail.

Using your sense of smell, notice any aromas or scents.

Are you able to notice any tastes as you walk? Can you taste the air?

Now using your sense of touch, notice the solidity of the earth beneath your feet.

With openness and curiosity, notice any sensations, thoughts or feelings that arise, without lingering on anything in particular.

You can mindfully walk anywhere outside while walking to work or school,or while walking through the grocery store.

Benefits Of Mindful Walking

1. It helps to lower stress: We all know that exercise can help to reduce stress, but mindful walking has been proved to be an extremely effective stress deterrent. I have had to put this into action plenty of times over the years.

2. Improves your mood: In addition to the physiological effects of exercise, which include the release of endorphins, increased levels of feel-good chemicals in the brain, and an increase in core temperature, we also experience a sense of accomplishment when we complete a task, especially when it is something that is beneficial to us. We feel better after experiencing these sentiments, which is why it's a great thing to do around lunchtime. Instead of returning to your desk feeling depressed or stuffed (after eating too much lunch), you'll feel lighter in mind, body, and spirit.

3. It reconnects you with your body: Because we spend so much of our time sitting, many of us have lost the connection with our bodies that was normal before. Walking mindfully on a regular basis gives you the opportunity to notice and feel every sensation in your body as it moves through the environment in which you are walking. Walking, breathing, and noticing are all activities that we take for granted, but when we pay attention to them, we realize just how marvelous it all is.

How to Take a Mindful Walk

Location: Where you head isn't important, just set out on a route that will take at about ten to fifteen minutes to walk. If you have thirty minutes or even an hour to spare, that's even better - but don't allow time to be a hindrance.

Before you begin, consider the following: If at all feasible, it's preferable to dress in clothes that make you feel comfortable and shoes that are easy to walk in so that you may remain as relaxed as possible. Consider taking a few deep breaths before you begin walking, and then do a quick check-in with yourself to see how you're feeling — scan your body and pay attention to what's happening. Check your breathing as well, and try to slow this down. Is there any kind of tension anywhere? Try to 'ground' yourself as well, which is to feel your feet firmly planted on the street or ground beneath your feet. What are your current feelings? It's important to take these feelings into consideration, but don't get caught up in them; instead, acknowledge them and watch them as if you were a third person looking in on yourself.

Start your walk by: Take it easy and enjoy the ride. At first, you could be self-conscious about your appearance, but don't worry, no one is watching, and this will allow you to concentrate more easily on the experience rather than how you appear. As you walk, pay close attention to the physical feelings you are experiencing. Pick one item, such as your breath or your pace, and focus on it. Is there any wind on your face or in your hair? Do you have any sense of the elements around you? Is it sunny outside, and can you feel the warmth of the sun on your skin? What sounds do you think you're hearing? Again, don't focus on them; instead, simply observe them briefly and return your attention to your breath. Concentrate on one item for thirty seconds to one minute at a time. After that, move on to the next concentration point.

When you've finished walking, take a time to notice your breath once more and perform another rapid body scan before continuing. How are you feeling right now? Your thoughts are more organized, and your body is less stressed. Do you feel more relaxed?

Experiment with this daily for three days in the first week and see how things change and how much simpler it becomes to enter into your mindful walks after that.

"Walk as if you are kissing the Earth with your feet."

— **Thich Nhat Hanh**

Mindful Drinking

Mindful drinking is about being aware of your surroundings and present in your decisions. The ultimate goal is to have a positive relationship with alcohol.

"We're not talking about abstinence unless you want to," mindful drinking is not intended for persons who have alcohol use disorders.

Mindful drinking is the concept of being deliberate in your decisions when it comes to alcohol consumption. It gives you the ability to make a deliberate decision rather than being swept along with the current of events.

It all comes down to adjusting the conversation you have with yourself. Drinking is socially accepted and, in certain cases, almost expected in today's society. Drinking is embedded in our culture in the same way that eating birthday cake on your birthday is engrained in our culture, as evidenced by cultural practices that include alcohol, such as a champagne toast at a wedding or going out for happy hour.

Benefits Of Mindful Drinking

1. GETTING A GOOD NIGHT'S SLEEP

It's no secret that alcohol can have a negative impact on your sleeping pattern, causing you to have difficulty falling asleep or remaining asleep during the night. Nothing is more unpleasant than waking up early for work or spending the day caring for children after a bad night's sleep. Why not try drinking less during the week and see if that helps? You can still indulge in a drink or two every now and then, but not too frequently.

2. GOODBYE TO HANGOVERS

Is it correct to say that no one enjoys a hangover? Is this correct? This was a no-brainer for us, to be honest. If giving up alcohol meant that we could wake up feeling refreshed and energized in the morning, we were all for it!

3. A CLEARER HEAD

This is true not only in terms of a hangover, but also in terms of your overall mental health. For a variety of reasons, some people find that consuming alcohol frequently causes them to experience feelings of anxiety. It's possible that you're concerned about something you said or did the night before. We recommend that you refrain from drinking for a time and instead enjoy a day (or night) to remember!

4. GLOWING SKIN

It's true that you could spend a fortune on a skincare routine recommended by your favorite Instagram blogger, or you could just try to cut back on the quantity of alcohol that you consume. The use of alcohol can dehydrate your skin, which isn't ideal, so we recommend giving it a shot and seeing if it works for you.

"You can't stop the waves, but you can learn to surf."

- Jon Kabat-zinn

Components Of Mindfulness

INTENTION

Your intention is the result you aim to achieve as a result of your mindfulness practice. You can be looking for stress relief, emotional harmony, or to find your actual nature. You should pay attention to the strength of your intention since it serves to encourage you to practice mindfulness on a regular basis and molds the quality of your mindful awareness, and it is crucial to identify what that is.

ATTENTION

In order to practice mindfulness, you must pay attention to your inner or outward experience in the present moment. Your focused attention is primarily formed by a variety of different methods of meditation, ranging from studying an item to engaging in a group exercise, among other things. The goal is to maintain complete concentration on whatever you are doing at any one time.

ATTITUDE

If you attempt to practice mindfulness while harboring a negative attitude about the practice, you will almost certainly fail. Aside from that, mindfulness entails paying attention to particular attitudes such as curiosity, acceptance, and kindness - towards the practice itself as well as the exercise that you are taking part in.

Mindfulness Therapy

Patients suffering from depression have found considerable benefit with mindfulness-based therapy, which is a type of cognitive behavioral therapy. This type of therapy is specifically meant to assist those who are suffering from chronic depression or other forms of dissatisfaction in their lives. It is a very unique type of therapy that provides a wide range of advantages and benefits.

How Does Mindfulness Therapy Work?

The way that mindfulness treatment works is that it teaches you to respond to situations in a different way than you would. People who are depressed frequently experience these sad states as a result of an automatic reaction. During the course of one's life, something terrible occurs, and the individual is forced into a depressive mood as a result of this incident. In order to be effective, mindfulness-based therapy must demonstrate to the patient how to respond when these occurrences occur.

This procedure is referred to as mindfulness-based cognitive therapy in the medical community. It entails altering your perception of the manner in which events are taking place.In place of instinctively reacting to events in your life, you might learn to just observe them and take note of their significance. It is critical to refrain from reacting to incoming stimuli as soon as they are received. As an alternative, you can simply accept and observe what is taking place.

It enables patients to accept what is going on in their lives rather than making impulsive decisions about it as a result of their experiences. Many people who are prone to depressive episodes react negatively to circumstances, and they frequently resort to self-criticism or end up feeling genuinely sad as a result of their reactions. When patients are able to make use of mindfulness therapy, they might begin to see things from a more objective perspective. It is possible to take a more measured approach and consider the problem as a whole rather than immediately reacting with negative feelings.

Of course, achieving this goal may not be straightforward at first. It is something that provides patients with the opportunity to alter their perspective on the world, although it is usually best accomplished with the assistance of a therapist. Patients can be guided through mindfulness therapy by a therapist, which can help them avoid the mistakes that can lead to depression. Once the patient has demonstrated progress and has learned how to alter their mental process, it becomes possible to employ these techniques in order to avoid going into a depressed frame of mind.

Studies have demonstrated that mindfulness-based cognitive treatment strategies can be effective in achieving beneficial outcomes. Patient responses to these treatments have been more rapid, and the treatments have assisted in the improvement of the lives of many people who suffer from depression. A number of research studies have been conducted to determine the viability of this treatment technique. All of them have discovered that mindful treatment is effective and has a long track record of success.

If standard counselling and treatment methods have not been effective for you, then mindfulness-based cognitive therapy may be a useful option for you to explore more. Many patients have indicated that it has aided their development, and some have reported that it has made it easier to avoid relapse. One of the most major difficulties associated with severe depression is that it can recur after a period of time. There has been a reduction in relapses in depressed states among patients who have used mindfulness-based therapeutic methods.

In most cases, the purpose of mindfulness-based cognitive therapy treatment programs is to educate the patient on what depression is really like. A therapist will work side by side with you to help you gain a better understanding of what depression is on a more fundamental level. They can collaborate with you in order to identify the factors that contribute to your spells of depression. The treatments will also assist you in determining why you have been caught in these depressive episodes for such a lengthy period of time.

Once things have been objectively assessed, it will be much easier to come up with a reasonable strategy for avoiding depression in the future. It is through mindfulness treatment that you will be able to recognize that there is a link between your despair and your unrealistic expectations. In many cases, individuals set themselves up to be too hard on themselves, which results in serious mental anguish.

Using Mindfulness Therapy Effectively

You will be happier if you use mindfulness treatment properly, which will help you lead a more fulfilling life. Suffering from depression is a major health problem that can put you in a difficult situation. Fortunately, this therapy style can benefit you in a variety of practical ways. As previously said, people have a tendency to evaluate themselves severely, which can result in episodes of sadness.

Uncovering where you are going wrong with the support of a mindfulness-based cognitive therapist is going to be quite beneficial. It is frequently your cognitive processes that are the root cause of these severe depressed episodes. Having self-conscious thoughts about not being good enough or feeling like you are not as capable as others will hold you back in life.

Meditation therapists will work with you to help you stop comparing yourself to others' accomplishments and instead focus on your own. Likewise, you should avoid placing yourself in situations where you are always under pressure or overloaded with tasks.

When you are under constant pressure, it is tough to preserve your happiness. Collaborating with your therapist to better understand the various triggers and factors in your life that can lead to depression is critical. They will be able to talk things through with you in order to assist you in seeing the positive aspects of life once more. People suffering from depression frequently lose sight of what is actually important in their lives. If mindful therapy may assist you in re-establishing a connection with what brings you happiness, it will be well worth your time.

One of the most significant advantages of this therapy method is the improvement in one's ability to see the world clearly. Depression and overall misery might cause you to feel as if your vision is blurred at some points in time. Due to your impaired vision, you may make unwise decisions as a result of your impairment of vision. There is no reason for you to continue to lose touch with reality in this manner when there are mindfulness-based therapists available to assist you.

This sort of therapy is practiced by a large number of different therapists. It is only one of the therapy methods that have been shown to be beneficial in the treatment of severe depression. It may be required to use a combination of different therapy methods in order to achieve the greatest outcomes in some cases. In order to get your mental health back on track, your therapists and doctors may decide to combine this technique with additional methods such as drugs.

If you are experiencing depression, you should consider seeking professional assistance. Being engulfed in depression is a difficult situation for anyone to deal with. It's even more difficult when you believe you're on your own in the situation. Contacting a therapist now can help you make positive changes in your life, and it will be a beneficial experience in the process. I do want to also add that mindfulness can be implemented with physical therapy. Recently my son shared with me that one of his friends who we met, a nice young man, who helped us at one of our events with packing up our products, had a motorcycle accident that nearly killed him. My son visited him one day and spent hours hanging out with him and as he shared his story with us I thought of how grateful I was that he was still here on this earth and the road to healing would require "Mindful Physical Therapy" He has since been released from the hospital and is on his mindful healing journey.

Managing Anxiety With Mindfulness Therapy

Do not allow fear, worry, panic, painful memories get in the way of accomplishing what you desire. When I would hear someone advise anyone or myself of what not to do my first thought was how? I would find myself stressing over things that I could not change. When you have a desire to change things in your life, it leads you down a path of learning, researching, studying. The way to accomplish this is to combine mindfulness with acceptance to help change the relationship with and response to those anxious thoughts. Mindfulness Therapy combines the practice of mindfulness with therapeutic techniques helping one to become more aware of the present moment. Mindfulness allows one to hear the inner voice when you find yourself distracted with thoughts that are the cause of the anxiety.

Mindfulness For Children

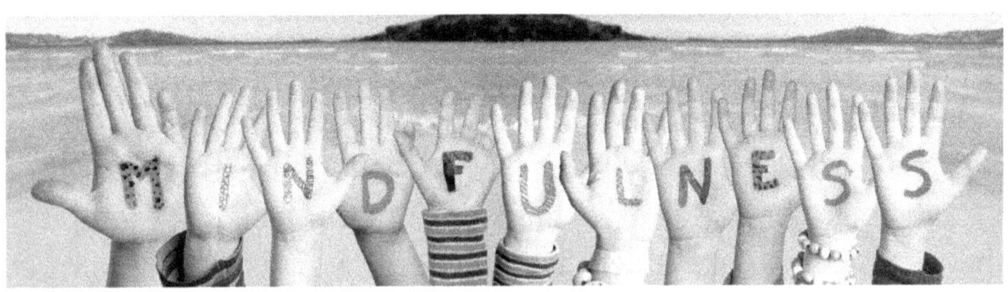

Children learn how to be present in their lives when they are taught mindfulness techniques. They gain the skills they need to build confidence, cope with stress, and relate to uncomfortable or challenging situations. The earlier we begin this process in their young lives, the higher the chance we have of assisting them in developing resilience as well as developing and refining their mindfulness practice as they mature.

It is also possible to teach mindfulness to children, which can help them develop three important abilities that are established in early childhood: paying attention and recalling information, switching back and forth between tasks, and behaving appropriately with others. These abilities are collectively referred to as executive functions, and they are required for more advanced tasks such as planning, reasoning, problem-solving, and maintaining favorable social connections.

We are confronted with adversity from the minute we are born. Infants experience hunger and fatigue. Toddlers are challenged with language and self-control issues. And when youngsters go through puberty and onto the stage of teenagerhood, life becomes increasingly challenging. Building relationships, navigating school, and asserting one's independence — the very stuff of growing up — all produce difficult conditions for children at some point in their development.

Mindfulness can be an effective approach for reducing anxiety and increasing happiness at every stage of development.

Benefits Of Mindfulness For Children

1. Cognitive Benefits

Teaching children mindfulness can have a positive impact on their cognitive abilities, specifically their ability to conduct executive tasks. When it comes to paying attention, switching focus, organizing information, recalling specifics, and engaging in planning, the executive functions are accountable for a person's ability to do so.

When a mindfulness program was implemented in a school for a period of eight weeks, we discovered that the students involved showed significant improvements in regulating their behaviors and focusing on the task at hand compared to a group of students that did not participate in the program.

Additionally, pupils who participated in a 24-week mindfulness program outperformed their peers in attention-based activities at their elementary school. In the same way, preschoolers who participated in a mindfulness curriculum performed better on academic performance assessments. Aside from that, they demonstrated more improvement in areas that are predictive of future academic achievement.

2. Emotional Benefits

Emotional health, often known as a positive sense of well-being, is a critical component of a child's development and success. Not only is it the foundation of mental health, but it may also be used to prevent mental health concerns such as: Anxiety, Stress\Depression, Problems with one's self-esteem, Social contacts have become more effective.

Overall, being attentive or engaging in mindfulness exercises can not only assist students in managing stress, but they can also improve their overall sense of well-being as a result. For example, students who participated in a mindfulness program were more likely to report feeling hopeful than those who did not. Meanwhile, I discovered that preteens who participated in a mindfulness and stress-reduction program reported feeling calmer, getting better sleep, and having a greater sense of well-being.

3. Social Advantages

A student's inability to interact and communicate with others may result in difficulties in learning, understanding, and school climate.

Mindfulness programs, on the other hand, have been found to strengthen these abilities and result in favorable outcomes in the classroom.

For example, mindfulness practices in an elementary school can result in increased involvement in classroom activities.. Meanwhile, a mindfulness program in a high school helped pupils develop mutual regard and concern for one another while also improving the overall climate of the school.

4. Other Benefits

In addition, mindfulness has been demonstrated to help children and teens better regulate their emotions, as well as to feel compassion and empathy for others. It is also commonly regarded as a helpful treatment for persons of all ages who are dealing with aggression, Attention Deficit Hyperactivity Disorder (ADHD), or other mental health issues such as anxiety. In addition, it can be utilized to relieve the painful consequences of bullying.

The practice of mindfulness can also be used to improve one's self-concept, increase one's planning skills, and manage one's impulses. Mindfulness can also help schools minimize the number of visits to the principal's office, reduce the amount of school bullying, and boost attendance if it is implemented properly in the setting of schools.

The overall goal of mindfulness is to encourage children and teenagers to reflect on their own thoughts and actions while also learning how to make more informed decisions. The objects in their environment are no longer causing people to react, but rather they are prompting them to behave in a thinking and purposeful manner.

"The mind is everything. What you think you become." ***- Buddha***

Smile
CLOUD GAZING
Exercise
Spend time with nature
Breathe
Walk BAREFOOT
Open Mind
RELAX
RELAX
RELAX
MINDFULNESS
FORGIVE
FORGIVE
FORGIVE
POSITIVE THINKING
Plant
Cook
Chat with friends
<listen>
Take a bath

Mindful Exercises For Kids

Mindful Coloring	**Balloon Breathing**	**Turtle Time stillness**	**Mindful walking**	**Gratitude Jar or Journal**
Choose a coloring page. Color slowly, paying attention to the colors, lines, and how it feels. Breathe while coloring. **Where:** At home as a calming activity, or during school free time. **Benefits:** Encourages present-moment focus and	Sit or stand comfortably. Imagine your belly is a balloon. Inhale slowly through the nose and imagine the balloon inflating. Exhale slowly and imagine it deflating. Repeat for 5 breaths. **Where:** Quiet time at home, before a test	Curl up like a turtle in your shell or sit cross-legged. Close your eyes or gaze down. Focus on breathing quietly. Stay still and silent for 1–2 minutes. **Where:** Transition times, when feeling overwhelmed. **Benefits:** Helps reset energy and increases	Walk slowly across the room or hallway. Pay attention to how your feet feel, the pressure, and the sounds. Try walking in silence for 2 minutes. **Where:** School hallway, backyard, or home living room. **Benefits:** Grounds attention in	Write or draw 1–3 things you're thankful for each day. Place them in a jar or journal. **Where:** Morning or bedtime routine, or at the end of the school day. **Benefits:** Builds a positive mindset and emotional resilience.

Mindful Coloring	Balloon Breathing	Turtle Time stillness	Mindful walking	Gratitude Jar or Journal
relaxation.	at school. **Benefits:** Calms nerves and helps with body awareness.	self-control.	the body and environment.	

Mindfulness and Online Safety for Kids

Mindfulness isn't just about calming the mind — it's also about *awareness*. When kids practice being mindful online, they learn to pause before clicking, scrolling, or sharing. It helps them notice what's happening, recognize potential risks, and make thoughtful choices instead of reacting impulsively.

Encourage children to:

- **Pause and think** before posting or responding.
- **Notice their feelings** when reading messages or seeing content online.
- **Ask for help** if something feels uncomfortable or unsafe.
- **Set boundaries** with screen time to stay balanced and present.

By practicing mindfulness, kids develop both **self-awareness** and **digital awareness**, creating safer and healthier online habits.

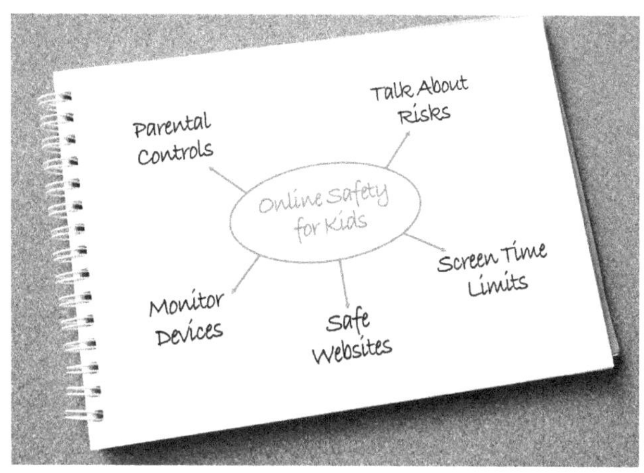

Understanding The Core Skills Of Mindfulness

"What" Mindfulness Skills

The "What Skills" are done one at a time, rather than all together. It means what we do when being mindful.

Observe

The first of these is Observe. The observer skill is just the ability to pay attention to what you are experiencing.

Simply observing your experience and acting on it without passing judgment. That may be your experience of your thoughts, it could be your experience of your emotions, it could be your five senses, or it could be something else entirely.

Whatever it is, you're noticing them, and you're doing it in a way that allows you to maintain a small amount of separation from them, noticing them without judgment, without reaction, and without feeling compelled to do or alter anything in response to them.

Describe

Your ability to describe what you have observed is mindfulness skill.

You're putting your thoughts into words. It might be that after noticing a thought, you express it by saying something like, "I notice the notion that I'm hungry." Take note of the thought that I am nervous; take note of the thought that when I am anxious, my heart rate increases and my chest feels tight."

Using specialized language to describe something.

You could do this by speaking aloud to a friend or family member. You can end up doing it to yourself. Perhaps by keeping a notebook of your thoughts.

In theory, when you explain and put words to your experience, you are allowing yourself to pay attention to it, and allowing yourself to process it in a different manner.

Participate

The third skill is the ability to participate.

When you put your whole heart and soul into anything, you've achieved success. As far as being actively involved in whatever is going on, it is more active.

A game you're playing, a job, or spending time with a friend or family member are all examples of what you can do to relax. In order to do this, you must put away any and all distractions, including your phone and other personal belongings. You must then concentrate on and participate fully in whatever activity you are engaged in at the time.

One way to ensure you are present is to set an intention before you start. Ask yourself:

Why am I doing this?

How do I want to feel after?

an example would be "I want to feel as if I am present and in the know of what is happening" or " I want to be attentive to my breath"

An observation has been that slowing down allows us time to notice more whether it's eating, walking or coloring. If we try doing it 20-50% slower than usual it will reduce the auto pilot behavior. If you also describe what you are noticing silently or aloud it helps. An example would be:

"I'm breathing in… I feel cool air in my nose" it helps to engage your thinking brain and keeps you present. This is a method I use frequently to keep me present. Refocus when your mind wanders, it is normal for the mind to wander and when it does notice it without judgement and bring your attention back to your breath, sound or sensation, we refer to this as a bicep curl for your attention, LOL. I am attempting to ***not*** add things like LOL in this fourth book but could not resist. Use the tools being provided to help you to participate.

'How' Mindfulness Skills

Now, these three 'How skills', are ones that we do all together. It's how we do mindfulness. Whereas the What skills, you might do one at a time, the how skills, we want to try to have those qualities present all the time.

Non-judgemental Stance

This one is difficult because we are accustomed to categorizing things as "good" or "bad." This ability, on the other hand, assists us in reducing our judgments and focusing on the facts. If you notice you're experiencing tightness and discomfort in your chest as a result of anxiety, you can say to yourself: "I'm feeling dreadful. This is quite embarrassing. It seems like everyone is staring at me, which is further aggravating my already bad mood."

In contrast, a non-judgmental perspective would be: "My chest feels constricted, and it's making it difficult to breathe."

Maintaining One's Concentration

One task at a time is recommended. This one is difficult for us because we live in a culture of multitaskers. However, it is critical to put this into practice. If you're going to be watching TV, then just watch TV. Don't use your phone to play a game or look through Twitter at the same time. Only eat dinner if you're going to eat dinner. Keep your attention on what you are doing at the moment and avoid distracting yourself with something else.

Effectiveness

It's okay to switch things around if something isn't working or is making you feel worse. It is perfectly acceptable to let go of something that no longer serves you.

Tips On Practicing Mindfulness

Mindfulness has three main elements that help with the practice of it: mind, emotions and body. Understanding these makes the use of mindfulness much simpler and easier.

Mindful Emotions

This is an area that I am still working on and realize it is a daily practice of awareness. Being such a patient person and realizing I can get stretched too thin. When my emotions come forth the tone of my voice shifts. I have to be mindful of what I am projecting. Know thyself, as there are times when my voice shifts and it is not connected with any type of negative emotion but simply concentrating. Being human, we will all have emotions, we are allowed to feel and express ourselves but oftentimes we are doing this without having an awareness that we could impact the energy in a space and make it shift into what could feel negative.

When practicing mindfulness, one of the most important things to become aware of is one's own emotions. Emotions can be draining and cause us to lose our concentration easily. Mindfulness, emotional intelligence, and maintaining healthy relationships can all be enhanced by being conscious of our feelings and reactions to circumstances.

Begin with these first six guidelines to help you on your journey to mindfulness. They provide an excellent beginning place for learning about the fundamentals of mindfulness and emotional intelligence, respectively.

Relaxed Attention

No matter how you're feeling bored, sad, irritated, angered or frustrated, pay relaxed attention to the emotion, as if you were seeing it from the outside. This has the potential to relieve unpleasant emotions and assist you in being more peaceful.

Keep a daily journal.

Writing can be a good way to start your day or a good way to end your day. Pay attention to the sensory subtleties. Alternatively, you may write about your life as a passive observer. As you check in with your emotions and thoughts on the page, this will assist you in limiting your judgments. It can also aid in the awareness of one's own emotions.

Repeat a Positive Affirmation.

It's quite simple to get sucked into a negative stream of thought. A wonderful method to counteract this is to repeat a positive affirmation over and over. The concentration on repetition is a mindful technique that also has the added benefit of making you feel more upbeat in your day to day activities.

Develop mindful interpersonal relationships.

Despite the fact that mindfulness is a very introspective exercise, it has been shown to have a good impact on our interpersonal connections. Consider the things you can do to help others. Even the smallest acts of kindness can have a positive impact on your relationships and help you develop greater compassion.

Pay attention to what others are saying.

Even if the person with whom you're conversing is the most uninteresting person you've ever encountered, they provide a great situation in which to practice attentive speaking. Instead of analyzing and criticizing what they are saying, try mindfully listening to them and paying relaxed attention to what they are saying instead.

Take a look at people.

One of the most effective ways to improve a relationship is to put your full attention on someone and look at them with sincere interest. Maintain eye contact with them, yet softly allow your gaze to drift away from their face at times. Try gazing without making any snap judgments. This is something that develops through time, just like any other mindfulness ability.

Mindful Body

Focusing on the body and physical abilities is an essential part of mindfulness. For those that find it difficult to practice mind or emotion focused habits this may be easier. During covid I met a young lady who promoted body positivity and I loved the confidence she displayed. It brought me a sense of joy and helped me to embrace my own flaws.

Focus on the body

A great element of mindfulness is that you don't even need to stop what you're doing to practice it. Whether it's the tap of your fingers on the keyboard, the posture of your back as you sit at your desk or the placement of your feet on the floor, you can gently bring your attention to your physical sensations. This will stop your mind from spiralling into the future or from over-analysing what you're doing.

Body scan

A body scan entails listening to the tensions in your body, focusing on them, and then releasing them, either by movement or just the focus of your mind. Don't allow your mind to analyse why you are tense, just enjoy the sense of relaxation and release. The Body scan has been mentioned a couple of times, by now you may have tried the body scan using the details provided within that section of the book.

Breathing

It's no secret that focusing on breathing is a great way to calm you down if you're stressed, but don't wait until then. To help you focus, practice breathing in through your nose and out through your mouth. If this proves difficult, countdown breaths from twenty. It may seem too easy, but it will help get rid of those distracting thoughts.

Exercise

Often, when we work out, we try to distract ourselves from what we're doing. A great way to become fully aware during an exercise routine is to have a purpose and plan like weight-loss and 3 kilometres. Try to slow down. This will help with awareness of what you're doing. Throughout remind yourself to breathe and focus on your breathing. Exercising mindfully also reduces the chance of injury. See the section on mindful eating and walking.

We have so many areas we could focus on when it comes to our bodies, keep in mind that mindfulness is not about being perfect, it is about showing up with curiosity and care. One area that I recently discovered that helps me in a tremendous way is my posture.

Mindful Posture

Sit or stand with your back straight (not stiff) shoulders relaxed, and eyes either closed or softly focused. A strong posture supports focused attention. I have asked these questions of myself after my "mindful posture"

How did it feel?

What did I notice?

How much was my mind wandering or focused?

It is a confidence booster for sure.

Mindfulness Meditation Techniques

Mindfulness meditation can be a great help for you in achieving mindfulness.

Mindfulness meditation is a mental training technique that teaches you to slow down racing thoughts, let go of negativity, and calm both your mind and body. A combination of mindfulness and meditation, which can be defined as a mental state characterized by complete concentration on "the present" in order to acknowledge and accept your thoughts, feelings, and sensations without judgment, is employed in this technique.

Mindfulness meditation techniques can vary, but in general, mindfulness meditation entails deep breathing and awareness of one's own body and thoughts. It is not necessary to use any props or prepare anything before beginning to practice mindfulness meditation (no need for candles, essential oils, or mantras, unless you enjoy them). It takes nothing more than a comfortable location to sit, three to five minutes of free time, and a judgment-free attitude in order to get started on your journey.

How to Practice Mindfulness Meditation

Learning mindfulness meditation is straightforward enough to practice on your own, but a teacher or program can also help you get started, particularly if you're practicing meditation for specific health reasons. Here are some simple steps to help you get started on your own. Book three of this series is all about meditation. If you want to further your knowledge as it relates to meditation, add the book into your library.

Get Comfortable

Find a quiet and comfortable place. Sit in a chair or on the floor with your head, neck, and back straight but not stiff. It's also helpful to wear comfortable, loose clothing so you're not distracted. But being that this practice can be done anywhere for any amount of time, a dress code is not required.

Consider a Timer

While it's not necessary, a timer (preferably with a soft, gentle alarm) can help you focus on meditation and forget about time—and eliminate any excuses you have for stopping and doing something else.

Since many people lose track of time while meditating, it can also ensure you're not meditating for too long. Be sure to also allow yourself time after meditation to become aware of where you are and get up gradually.

While some people meditate for longer sessions, even a few minutes every day can make a difference. Begin with a short, 5-minute meditation session and increase your sessions by 10 or 15 minutes until you are comfortable meditating for 30 minutes at a time.

Focus on Breathing

Become aware of your breath, attuning to the sensation of air moving in and out of your body as you breathe. Feel your belly rise and fall as the air enters your nostrils and leaves your nostrils. Pay attention to the temperature change when the breath is inhaled versus when it's exhaled.

Notice Your Thoughts

The goal is not to stop your thoughts but to get more comfortable becoming the "witness" to the thoughts. When thoughts come up in your mind, don't ignore or suppress them. Simply note them, remain calm, and use your breathing as an anchor. Imagine your thoughts as clouds passing by; watch them float by as they shift and change. Repeat this as often as you need to while you are meditating.

Give Yourself a Break

If you find yourself getting carried away in your thoughts—whether with worry, fear, anxiety, or hope—observe where your mind went, without judgment, and just return to your breathing. Don't be hard on yourself if this happens; the practice of returning to your breath and refocusing on the present is the practice of mindfulness.

Tips to Practice Mindfulness in Daily Life

With mindfulness meditation, it becomes easier to incorporate awareness into your regular life—especially on those days when your schedule is too hectic to take out a minute for yourself. Mindfulness meditation is one way, but there are several possibilities for mindfulness practice in everyday activities and duties.

Brushing your teeth: Feel your feet on the floor, the brush in your hand, and your arm moving up and down.

Doing dishes: Savor the feeling of the warm water on your hands, the look of the bubbles, and the sounds of the pans clunking on the bottom of the sink.

Doing laundry: Pay attention to the smell of the clean clothes and the feel of the fabric. Add a focus element and count your breaths as you fold laundry.

Driving: Turn off the radio—or put on something soothing, like classical music. Imagine your spine growing tall, find the half-way point between relaxing your hands and gripping the wheel too tightly. Whenever you notice your mind wandering, bring your attention back to where you and your car are in space.

Exercising: Instead of watching television while on the treadmill, try focusing on your breathing and where your feet are as you move.

Getting kids ready for bed: Get down to the same level as your kids, look in their eyes, listen more than you talk, and savor any snuggles. When you relax, they will too.

Being intimidated by the prospect of establishing a mindfulness meditation practice might be discouraging, but it's vital to realize that even a few minutes of meditation each day can be useful. Being present for even a few minutes at a time can have enormous rewards. Although you may not practice it every day, it is a discipline that you can return to whenever you feel the need.

"To be mindful is to be aware of your thoughts, your body, and your surroundings in the present moment without judgement."

-Ruth Baer

Mindfulness In Relationships

There are a variety of relationship types that exist and some of them can be complicated. Any relationship takes two people working together — a shared willingness to build it, an open mind that understands both people and circumstances change, and the intention to speak about the relationship in a constructive way. This means focusing on what you want rather than what is lacking, and avoiding adding fuel to the fire by speaking negatively about the other person. When that person is in your presence, not giving the side eye to others in that space or giving off bad energy. As you can see, relationships are complicated at any age, and no one enjoys dealing with someone they feel doesn't like them.Life is short, so we keep it moving and build those relationships that matter most and the ones that will make a difference in positive, powerful ways. In this section I want to discuss mindfulness in intimate relationships first and then friendships later. Relationships can become boring if you allow them. They can lose the spark or excitement and this is where you will find yourself lacking the desire that is necessary to keep the relationship fresh. This is why we must have an awareness of how mindfulness can help us to remain actively engaged for many years to come.

The Married Life

Mindful listening is an absolute for couples, because when we stop listening some would say it's a sign of trouble. I call it a lack of mindfulness during conversations. We may all be guilty of this. If you've ever used your phone while talking with a loved one—checking social media, reading emails, or playing a game—you may see it as multitasking. Your partner, however, may experience it as distracting or frustrating, particularly when they feel unheard and need to repeat themselves. You may nod in agreement, they run off to make a decision and you realize you heard nothing that was being presented to you due to being distracted and this could cause an issue.

Many of us grew up in households where we witnessed our parents' relationships and we formed our opinions based on what we saw and heard. Keep all that you have seen and heard that has been helpful and that has worked for you but we must let go of all that we seen and heard that was not good benign sure to not bring this into your current relationship, the good news is that it is not too late to consider the benefits of mindfulness and develop this practice. If you are married and out of the honeymoon phase, mindfulness is a key element to add into the relationship and can help to make the relationship feel fresh and everlasting. Be sure to add in date nights of some sort that will help you to remain connected to one another. Oftentimes once in a relationship for a while couples become comfortable and can be easily moved to no longer dating.

Think of that exciting feeling you had when you were new, things were fresh and you were getting to know one another. Keep the lines of communication open and be mindful of what is important to the two of you as a couple. Once we can fall into the routine of life we cannot forget that romance is a part of intimacy and helps us to stay connected with our partners. Be mindful not to allow work and other outside influences pull you away so frequently that you outgrow each other. Find new things that you can do together. The key is to share the experience of life together in as many positive ways as possible. Mindfulness asks us to see reality clearly, not sugarcoat it. I have found this helps my husband and I to keep open and honest communications with each other.

Mindful Relationship Fun Date Ideas:

If you have children who require care during date nights, plan ahead to minimize last minute cancellations due to no child care in place. Dating is important in relationships. The ideas below may not be new to you and may simply jolt you into a new idea and it may be new for some the goal is to reignite "mindfulness" into the relationship. Think back to when you were new in your relationship, did it make you smile? When you think of your relationship during the highs, what was it that made the relationship amazing for both of you? We will explore ideas for date night, this can be after your kids have gone to bed, putting forth effort is key.

All too often we hear jokes about marriage as if being married is a bad thing where "I Do" means we are now stuck unhappily ever after together and that it's only a piece of paper that holds them together (paper, which also includes their financial obligations) and they fall into a loveless marriage. A marriage can be filled with love, happiness, fun, as well as respect for one another and no it's not the fairytale because people are people and as long as we are mindful of this, while they can still get under our skin from time to time it will not be as annoying when we are mindfully present in relationship we have better communication with our partners. Here are ideas you may want to explore.

"*Your task is not to seek for love, but merely to seek and find all the barriers within yourself that you have built against it.*" **- Rumi**

Ideas For Date Night

Visit a new place "a day trip" just the two of you.	Start a small project together. This can include going to a craft store together	Take a cooking class together and then make each' others favorite dish	Make your anniversary a big deal by celebrating it. Plan ahead. Treat it with love and care
A themed movie night "80's" "90's Action, Love etc.	Paint night	Sound Therapy Art Therapy Coloring books	Sports event
Weekend getaway	Hiking, walking, bike riding, any outdoor activity, swimming	Farmers markets, swamp meets	Antique stores Museums, art displays
Go see your favorite band in concert, listen to music from the comfort of your home, singing and dancing	Live comedy event, be open to trying new things together regardless of how many years you have been married	Travel to a place you have dreamed of going. keep the romance alive	Both of you create a list of fun ideas and then swap lists. reading what each one wrote and selecting items off of each others list that you will do
Couples spa day	A day vacation where you both	Join an organization	Picnic in the backyard, at

find 3 good things about each other you observed throughout the day and share it with one another at the end of the day	fly to a city that is about an hour flight for the day and fly back	such as a humanitarian	a park or while on a road trip
Game night pull out your favorite games and play. Monopoly, scrabble, spades, Uno, Skippo to name a handful. There are way too many to name	Pickle ball Tennis Golf Horse Back riding Roller Skating Create podcast	Bookstore Couples retreats Vacation Short trips Couples photo shoot	Live Play Live entertainmen t Live bands Jazz music Live opera

- Put your cell phones away when you are each sharing about your day.

What do you enjoy most about each other?

How often do you share this with one another?

Couples Guided Visualization

Lay down on your back side by side with both of your heads pointing in the same direction. Hold hands, close your eyes.

Take a deep breath in and slowly exhale out of your open mouth.

Take 2 more breaths simply in your natural rhythm of breathing.

Imagine that you are both a part of the sun shining in the sky and that you have the power to look like anything you want, you can change shapes and do all sorts of tricks, flips and although you are both the sun you are two individuals and can also collide into one being.

Picture both of you bright, powerful, happy and shining your light. Picture the two of you dancing, bouncing into yourselves and into one, back and forth.

As a couple discuss how this mindful exercise made you feel. Was it difficult to imagine? Did the exercise make you smile? did you allow you to feel a sense of closeness to your partner? Journal about your experience below.

Revisiting Boundaries in a relationship

Do you believe relationships should have boundaries placed on them?

Do you have your personal boundaries in place outside of your marriage?

In a relationship there are basic boundaries that should be set up and revisited throughout the relationship. Questions to ask yourself if my partner does not come home and spends the night out is this okay? and if so under what circumstances?

Are you in an open relationship and made aware of this? Being mindful of how our partners feel and being sure to communicate is important.

I often would hear people talking about Will Smith and Jada Pinkett's marriage and how it was all these things that no one would ever want in their relationship. Most of the people who speak on others' relationships do not always have their own intact just yet. While we may not agree on what other's relationships are or are not. Focus on what you want for your relationship. Be mindful that it takes two people to be in a relationship and they must both be mindful of each other in all that they do. Do what is going to be best for your soul. When we are in unhappy relationships it is considered as unhealthy and must be evaluated based on your mind, body and spirit. One way for you to connect with your partner is to learn about love languages. There is a popular book by Gary Chapman titled Love languages where the author shares the five love languages which is helpful in discovering your and your partners love language you each speak. This is also fun to learn together if possible.

Signs your boundaries need to be revisited

1. not being able to say no
2. allowing others to make decisions for your life
3. inability to notice when others cross boundaries
4. being intimate with someone just to make them happy
5. going against your values to please others

Remember:

Speak from the heart use "I feel instead of you always" statements. Be honest and gentle with your partner, sharing without blaming. Speak with intention to connect but not to win. An example: " I feel disconnected when we don't talk at night. I miss you." Offer loving touch with presence. When you hug, kiss or hold hands, slow it down.

These days we are often rushing. Allow your body language to say "I'm here" and pause the multi-tasking as we cannot multi-task love. It requires us to give our full attention. When you are hugging your partner try a 20 second hug as it releases oxytocin, the love hormone. I learned this from a couples coach and have observed this to be true.

It is important to have daily check-ins and weekly mindful dates. You can also create a morning or bedtime gratitude where you share one thing you appreciate about each other; this consistency builds trust and emotional safety.

Mindful Love Notes:

Write short, meaningful notes or messages
Share a memory, a compliment, or something you're grateful for.
Leave them in places your partner will find them (mirror, pillow, lunchbox)

Practice Acceptance:

Notice the urge to change or "fix" your partner.
Gently release judgment and choose compassion instead.
Love them as they are, not as they "should be"
Ask yourself: "Can I love this part of them too?"

Who can benefit from Mindfulness Therapy for couples?

Couples facing ongoing conflict or communication challenges.

Partners seeking deeper emotional intimacy and connection.

Those wanting to integrate mindfulness into their relationship as a preventive or growth practice.

Life Is Good Activity

Time: Five to Ten minutes

Supplies: Ball

1. You will sit across from each other and roll the ball to each other. When the ball comes to you, name one thing that's bothering you. Then roll the ball back and say, "life is good"

2. Example: I received a traffic ticket in the mail today costing $250.00….. roll the ball to another player or to your partner while saying "life is good" couples can use this to help them bring awareness into their relationships without having what is meant to be a helpful conversation turning into any one storming out of the room.

This game is not about pretending that challenges do not exist, we first acknowledge the challenge, then we reframe it by bringing awareness to the positive things in our lives as well. You can use variations to this exercise another example would be…. Name the thing that you are unhappy about and say something positive about the same topic and pass the ball. Example: I had a disagreement with my son today, now proceed to roll the ball and say, I still feel lucky to have my son in my life.

Three Good Things Activity

Three good things has been an activity I have added in nearly all of my journals as a part of gratitude, using variations of this. you can use this in your relationship directed towards each other. Example: Three things I enjoy about you and the other person shares three things with you. This is a great activity to implement at a time during challenging times in the relationship.

Mindful Breathing

Think of your breath as your built-in reset button. When you learn how to use it intentionally, you tap into a powerful tool for managing stress, shifting your energy, and strengthening your emotional resilience. In this section, I'll guide you through the essentials of mindful breathing and introduce several techniques you can use in real time—during tough conversations, before meetings, when you wake up, or whenever your mind begins to wander. This area has worked wonders for me.

Let's take a closer look by breaking down a variety of breathing techniques where you are applying mindfulness. This can be a fun exercise alone or in a group setting. Our breath is with us, helping to support us in our journey. Knowing the variety of ways to use your breath and practicing the breathing techniques is known as mindfulness breathing, let's break down the categories. I do want to clarify the difference between Mindful breathing and Breathwork.

Mindful Breathing is about (Awareness-Based / Gentle)

- **Focus:** Observing and connecting with the breath as it is — *without changing it dramatically.*

- **Examples:** 4-7-8 breathing, box breathing, flower breathing, counting breaths.

- **Purpose:** Presence, calm, grounding, self-regulation, and awareness of the present moment.

- **Approach:** Soft, intentional, and used as an anchor for mindfulness or meditation.

By now you may have heard or currently practice breathwork and are aware of the amazing benefits.

Breathwork is about (Energetic / Transformational)

- **Focus:** Uses specific breathing patterns to shift energy, clear emotions, or alter consciousness.

- **Examples:** Circular breathing, Wim Hof, rebirthing, holotropic breathwork.

- **Purpose:** Transformation, release, energy activation, or nervous system reset.
- **Approach:** Often structured, with stronger or longer breath cycles that intentionally move prana or chi through the body.

Now, let's focus on mindful breathing in this section. Our breath is an awesome tool.

Mindful Breathing Basics

Basic mindfulness meditation breath was touched upon earlier in the book but, I want to also add it here where all of the breathing techniques are grouped together.

Technique:

- Sit or lie down comfortably.
- Bring your full attention to your breath.
- Simply observe the inhale and exhale without changing it.
- When your mind wanders, gently return to the breath.

Benefits:

- Improves present-moment awareness
- Trains attention and focus
- Lowers stress and rumination
- Can reduce anxiety and depressive symptoms

Star Breathing

A visual and movement-based breathing technique that uses the points of a star to guide slow, rhythmic breaths. Perfect for children, adults, and anyone who needs a calming reset.

Technique

Trace or visualize the five points of a star with your finger or mind, breathing in and out as you move along each line.

Benefits

- Calms the nervous system
- Helps with emotional regulation
- Improves focus and concentration
- Creates predictable rhythm and structure (ideal for anxiety)
- Great for kids, corporate wellness, and grounding moments

How To

1. Hold up one hand like a star (fingers spread wide) *or* visualize a five-point star in your mind.
2. Place your finger at the bottom of your thumb or at one point of the star.
3. **Inhale** as you trace the line up to the top of the star point.
4. **Exhale** as you trace down to the next point.
5. Continue inhaling on the upward lines and exhaling on the downward lines as you move around the star.

6. Go all the way around the star, completing 5 breaths (one for each point).

7. Repeat 2–3 full stars or continue until you feel your body soften and settle

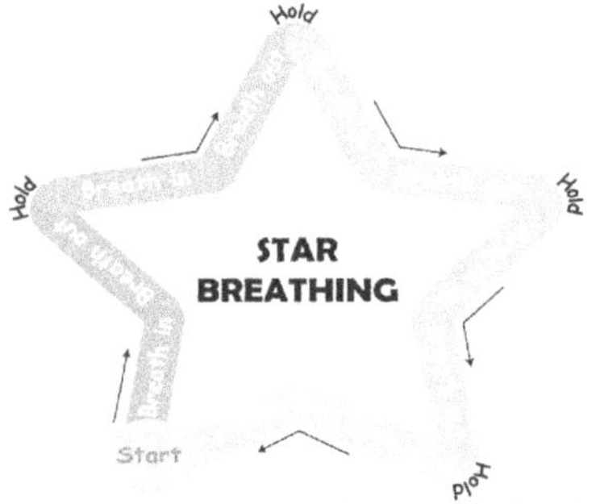

Infinity breathing also known as: Figure 8 breathing.

Technique:

- Visualize or trace the shape of an infinity symbol (a sideways figure 8).
- Inhale as you trace one half of the 8.
- Exhale as you trace the other half.
- Repeat for several cycles, breathing slowly and evenly.

Benefits:

- Calms the nervous system
- Promotes focus and concentration
- Encourages rhythmic, balanced breathing
- Helps integrate both hemispheres of the brain

INFINITY BREATHING

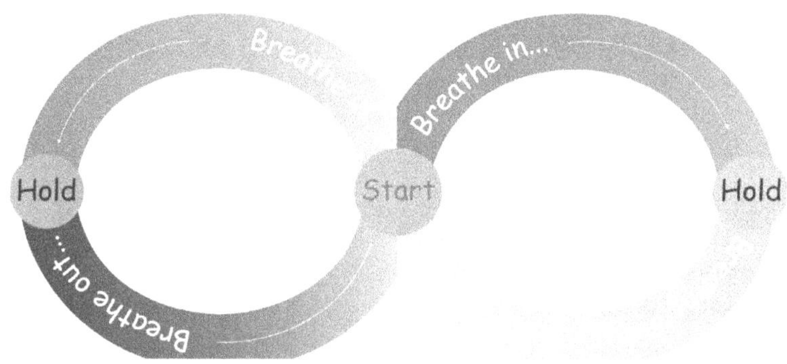

Flower breathing imagery-based breath

often used with children and adults alike.Inhale as if you're smelling a flower... exhale as if you're blowing the petals gently. I enjoy this exercise when I have a flower in my hand. Flower breathing purpose and energy align more directly with

Mindful breathing — cultivating calm and awareness rather than transformation or energy release.

Technique:

- Imagine holding a beautiful flower.
- Inhale deeply through the nose, as if smelling the flower.
- Exhale gently through the mouth like blowing on petals.
- Repeat slowly for 5–10 rounds.

Benefits:

- Induces calm and presence through visualization
- Enhances emotional regulation
- Promotes slow, deep breathing

- Can reduce anxiety and bring a sense of beauty and peace

Heart breathing is often used in HeartMath and coherence practices.

Technique:

- Place one or both hands over your heart.
- Inhale slowly into your heart space (about 4–6 seconds).
- Exhale slowly and fully (about 6 seconds).
- Imagine breathing in compassion, love, or calm.
- Do this for 2–5 minutes.

Benefits:

- Enhances emotional balance
- Supports heart-brain coherence
- Boosts feelings of self-compassion and empathy
- Can regulate blood pressure and stress hormones

Deep breath breathing is Foundational diaphragmatic breathing

Technique:

- Inhale deeply through the nose, expanding your belly, then ribs, then chest (3-part breath).
- Exhale slowly through the mouth.
- Try 4–6 seconds in, 6–8 seconds out.
- Practice for 1–3 minutes

Benefits:

- Activates the parasympathetic nervous system (rest-and-digest)
- Reduces tension and stress
- Enhances oxygen intake
- Grounds you in your body

Box breathing is used by Navy SEALs, athletes and professionals under pressure.

Box breathing — also known as **square breathing** — is one of the most powerful yet simple breath techniques for calming the mind and steadying the nervous system.
It's called "box" breathing because the breath is divided into four equal parts, forming a mental square: **inhale, hold, exhale, hold.**

Even though it's now commonly used in meditation and wellness circles, this technique has deep roots in **ancient yogic breath practices** and was later adapted and popularized by the **U.S. Navy SEALs**.
Why? Because it works — especially under pressure.

When Navy SEALs are in high-stress, high-stakes environments, they use box breathing to stay focused, lower adrenaline, and regulate their body's stress response.
The same practice that helps soldiers remain calm in combat can help us remain calm in the midst of our everyday battles — whether that's a difficult conversation, a busy workday, or simply a racing mind.

Technique:

- Inhale through the nose for 4 seconds
- Hold the breath for 4 seconds
- Exhale slowly through the mouth for 4 seconds
- Hold again for 4 seconds
- Repeat for 4–6 rounds.

Benefits:

- Boosts mental clarity and focus
- Reduces stress and anxiety
- Improves performance under pressure
- Regulates the breath rhythmically

While box breathing is often taught as a tactical or performance tool, at its heart, it's a mindfulness practice.
Each side of the "box" brings awareness to a different phase of the breath — inhaling, holding, releasing, and pausing.
That steady rhythm quiets the chatter of the mind and invites you back into the body, into the *now.*

> "Inhale focus.
> Hold stillness.
> Exhale tension.
> Hold peace."

Keep in mind, You can use box breathing anytime you feel your energy becoming scattered:

- Before a meeting or important conversation
- When your mind starts to race
- As a mini reset between tasks
- Or as part of your daily mindfulness ritual

The Navy SEALs may use it to steady themselves before action — but for us, it's a reminder that peace is not found in escaping the moment, but in *breathing through it.*

Leaf breathing

It is great for grounding and nature connection. Leaves represent **life, growth, renewal, and letting go**.

Just as a leaf absorbs sunlight and breathes in carbon dioxide to create oxygen — it gives life through its natural rhythm.

Technique:

- Imagine or trace the edge of a leaf with your finger.
- Inhale slowly as you trace one side.
- Exhale as you trace the other.
- Repeat with different leaves or visualizations.
- Can be done with real leaves or on printed leaf outlines.

Benefits:

- Encourages slow, conscious breathing
- Connects you with nature and grounding energy
- Great for kids and adults alike
- Promotes emotional regulation and calm

This is a practice that resonates with me very well. In the event you want to add in the practice of Leaf breathing, I have provided additional details below.

How to Practice Leaf Breathing

You can do this practice using a real leaf, an image, or simply your imagination.

1. **Find a leaf** — hold it in your hand or visualize one in your mind. Notice its color, texture, and unique shape.
2. **Trace the outline of the leaf slowly** with your finger or with your breath in your imagination.
3. As you **inhale**, trace up one side of the leaf — breathing in calm, peace, and awareness.
4. As you **exhale**, trace down the other side — letting go of tension, worry, or distraction.
5. Continue this gentle tracing for several rounds, allowing your breath to flow naturally and your attention to rest softly on the rhythm.

You can also repeat a simple affirmation as you breathe, such as:

Inhale calm, exhale release.
Inhale peace, exhale stress.
Inhale love, exhale fear.

Tree Breathing

A grounding technique that connects you with stability and balance.

Technique

Visualize yourself as a tree—rooted, steady—and use slow breaths paired with upright posture.

Benefits:

- Enhances stability and focus
- Reduces stress and emotional overwhelm
- Encourages patience and presence
- Supports balance in the body

How To

1. Stand tall with feet hip-width apart.
2. Imagine roots growing from your feet into the earth.
3. Inhale through your nose as you reach your arms upward like growing branches.
4. Exhale as you slowly lower your arms, keeping your "roots" strong.
5. Optional: Lift one foot to practice balance breathing (tree pose).
6. Repeat for 6–10 breaths.

Rainbow Breathing

A mindful, visual breathing technique great for grounding and uplifting energy.

Technique

Use a sweeping arm motion to trace an imaginary rainbow while syncing your breath with the movements.

Benefits:

- *Boosts mood and emotional balance*
- *Helps children and adults calm quickly*
- *Encourages creativity and visualization*
- *Harmonizes breath and movement*

How To

1. *Stand or sit with your arms down at your sides.*
2. *Inhale deeply while lifting both arms up and outward, tracing the arc of a rainbow over your head.*
3. *Exhale slowly as you bring your arms back down.*
4. *Imagine each breath painting a new color.*
5. *Repeat 5–7 rounds, visualizing a full rainbow.*

Hexagon Breathing

A structured breathing technique that uses a six-count pattern inspired by the six sides of a hexagon.

Technique

Trace or visualize a hexagon while breathing in specific timed segments.

Benefits:

- *Strengthens focus and mental clarity*
- *Reduces anxiety*
- *Helps regulate the nervous system*
- *Excellent for kids, trauma-sensitive settings, and corporate wellness*

How To

1. *Visualize or draw a hexagon in front of you.*

2. *Inhale for **3 counts** while imagining tracing the first side.*

3. *Hold for **3 counts** tracing the next side.*

4. *Exhale for **3 counts** tracing the next side.*

5. *Hold for **3 counts** tracing the next side.*

6. *Continue this pattern for all sides of the hexagon (full cycle = 6 segments).*

7. *Repeat 3–5 cycles.*

Alternative:

- *Inhale (side 1)*
- *Hold (side 2)*
- *Exhale (side 3)*
- *Hold (side 4)*
- *Inhale (side 5)*
- *Hold (side 6)*

Butterfly Breathing

A calming breath technique often paired with light self-hugging or gentle arm movements.

Technique

Cross your arms over your chest (as if giving yourself a gentle hug), place your hands on your upper arms or shoulders, and breathe slowly while lightly fluttering or tapping your hands like butterfly wings.

Benefits:

- *Soothes the nervous system*
- *Increases emotional regulation*
- *Creates a sense of safety and grounding*
- *Reduces anxiety and tension*
- *Encourages self-compassion*

How To

Sit or stand comfortably.
Cross your arms so your hands rest on opposite shoulders or upper arms.
Inhale slowly through your nose as your elbows rise slightly (like wings opening).
Exhale slowly as your elbows lower.
Optional: Add gentle alternating taps with your hands ("butterfly taps").
Repeat for 6–10 breaths

clarity
awakening
relaxation
alignment
spiritual
inner peace
strength
focus
meditation
wellness
tranquility
energy
body
serenity
peace
mind
mental
connection
grounding
stillness
inner strength
presence
lifestyle
breathing
concentration
balance
yoga
harmony
flexibility
selfcontrol
flow
calm
zen

Awareness meter

Used to help us notice how we're feeling. Fill in the meter below add emotions/words that resonate with you. This is a great exercise to use with children as well.

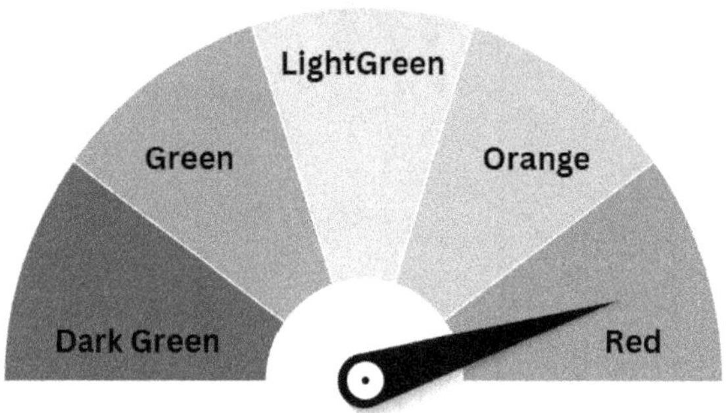

Color Mood Meanings Chart

Red — The Red Zone (Overwhelmed / Distressed)

- *Represents anger, frustration, sadness, or deep exhaustion.*
- *You may feel tense, triggered, or emotionally drained.*
- *This is your reminder to pause, breathe, and tend to yourself with compassion.*

Orange — Emotional Alert (Anxious / Uneasy)

- *Symbolizes worry, nervousness, restlessness, or irritation.*
- *You might feel off balance or uncertain, but still aware.*

- *This is your cue to slow down, ground yourself, and check in with your needs.*

Green — Balanced (Calm / Grounded)

- *Reflects emotional steadiness, peace, and mindful presence.*
- *You feel in flow — neither too high nor too low.*
- *You're able to breathe deeply, respond intentionally, and move through your day with ease.*

Light Green — Renewal (Hopeful / Healing)

- *Represents growth, optimism, and gentle self-compassion.*
- *You're emerging from difficult emotions, feeling lighter or more at peace.*
- *This shade reminds you that healing and progress are unfolding.*

Dark Green — Reflection (Withdrawn / Contemplative)

- *Symbolizes introspection, solitude, or deep emotional processing.*
- *You might feel quiet or inward, not necessarily sad — just reflective.*
- *This is your sign to nurture yourself, rest, and listen to your inner wisdom.*

Mindful Practice Tip

Check in with yourself daily to ask; *"What color am I today?"* Let's take a look at another important relationship.

The Relationship Between Mindfulness and Deconstruction

This is a very philosophical and psychological angle that most mainstream books don't touch on. Many people hear the word Ego and arrogance or pride. In mindfulness and psychology, the ego is much more than that. The ego is the part of the mind that creates a sense of "I," identity, and separation.It's not bad or something to eliminate — it's simply a structure we learn to observe. The goal is not to destroy the ego, but to understand it so it doesn't control our reactions. Ego is formed in many ways to protect us. Let's go deeper.

- **Mindfulness as a Tool for Deconstructing the Ego:** Explore how a consistent mindfulness practice can reveal the impermanent, constructed nature of the "self" or "ego." Instead of just observing thoughts, observe the *narrator* of the thoughts. Stepping back from your thoughts and watching them like an observer, not a character in the story, This can lead to a deeper sense of liberation from self-limiting beliefs and stories.
- **The "No-Self" Concept (Anatta):** Directly addressing the idea of "no-self" is a radical departure from Western psychology's focus on building a strong self. Seeing that thoughts, feelings, and sensations are not "mine" but simply phenomena arising and passing—can lead to profound freedom and compassion.

Integrating Mindfulness with Other Disciplines

- **Mindfulness and Stoicism:** Mindfulness and Stoicism intersect in their shared teaching that peace comes from accepting what lies beyond our control and directing our energy toward the one thing we can influence—our inner state.
- **Mindfulness and Narrative Therapy:** Narrative Therapy teaches that our lives are shaped by the stories we believe about ourselves. Mindfulness adds the ability to slow down and actually *see* those stories as they arise. Together, they allow us to identify the limiting narratives we've been living in and consciously rewrite them into ones that support growth, confidence, and healing.
- **Mindfulness and Systems Thinking:** Mindfulness and Systems Thinking complement one another by expanding our awareness beyond the individual self. Systems Thinking reminds us that we exist within multiple interconnected systems—family, work, community, society, and nature. Mindfulness strengthens our ability to observe how these systems influence our thoughts, emotions, and behaviors. When we become more aware of these connections, we begin to understand that our actions are never isolated; they create ripple effects that extend outward into the systems we are part of.

Exploring the "Shadow" Side of Mindfulness

Realistically, in life we all know there can be pitfalls and challenges in practicing mindfulness. Spiritual bypassing is something I have spoken about on a podcast, we cannot meditate our way out of uncomfortable emotions. It reminds me of toxic positivity.

The Trap of Spiritual Bypassing

While mindfulness is a powerful tool for healing and self-awareness, it can also be misused. This is known as **spiritual bypassing** — when someone uses spiritual practices like meditation, positive thinking, or "staying calm" to *avoid* facing uncomfortable emotions. This is toxic.

Instead of helping us move through pain, bypassing allows us to temporarily escape it. We may tell ourselves to "just breathe," "stay positive," or "let it go," when in truth, our inner world is asking to be felt, acknowledged, and understood.

Mindfulness is not about suppressing emotions.
It is not meant to silence your anger, numb your sadness, or gloss over your hurt.

Mindfulness invites you to gently **sit with what arises** — even when it's hard.
It asks you to witness your thoughts and feelings without judgment, without rushing to fix them or push them away.

When you practice true mindful presence, you:

- Allow your emotions to surface rather than burying them
- Honor your pain as part of the human experience
- Create space for healing instead of avoiding it
- Respond with compassion rather than denial

You learn that discomfort is not your enemy — it is often your teacher.

Mindfulness becomes a pathway to transformation when you choose honesty over avoidance, awareness over suppression, and self-compassion over forced calmness.

The goal is not to meditate the pain away.
The goal is to **be present with yourself**
— your joy, your grief, your anger, your fears —
and to let each emotion move through you in its own time.

This is how true healing happens.
This is how you grow into your higher self — not by bypassing the difficult parts of your journey, but by meeting them with courage, clarity, and love.

Advanced Mindfulness Challenges

Most books about mindfulness are not this detailed when it comes to providing a section on advanced mindfulness challenges. You may notice that this book goes deeper than most mindfulness resources. Many books stop at the basics, but my goal is to ensure that you are **fully supported** on every level of your journey — foundational, emotional, spiritual, and advanced.

Some of the practices may feel familiar, and a few concepts may sound similar to earlier sections. This is intentional.

Mindfulness is not a one-time lesson; it is a layered practice.
Each time you revisit a concept, you understand it differently — with more awareness, more maturity, and more clarity than before.

Rather than asking you to flip back to another chapter or search for earlier information, I chose to include everything you need *right where you need it.*
No "refer to chapter ___," no hunting for earlier explanations.
Just a smooth, continuous experience that honors your growth.

This book is designed to walk with you step by step, offering clarity, depth, and guidance without interruption.
The advanced challenges are included because I want you to feel **fully equipped** — not just informed, but empowered.

Every section, every repetition, and every expansion is here to support your evolution into your higher self with ease, confidence, and intention.

1. The Radical Self-Honesty Challenge

For one week, pause whenever you feel triggered and ask:
"What am I truly feeling, and what am I avoiding?"
Write down your honest answer — without softening it, spiritualizing it, or explaining it away.

This challenges the ego and deepens emotional clarity.

2. The Mindful Conflict Challenge

Choose one difficult conversation you've been postponing.
Before the conversation, practice mindful breathing for five minutes.
During the conversation, keep at least 10% of your attention on your body's sensations.

This builds emotional regulation and higher-self communication skills.

3. The Discomfort Sitting Practice

Set a timer for 5–7 minutes.
Sit with one uncomfortable feeling — frustration, sadness, anger, loneliness — without trying to fix it or change it.

Simply observe where it lives in your body and how it shifts.

This is an advanced antidote to spiritual bypassing.

4. The Awareness Expansion Walk

Take a 20–30 minute walk without your phone.
Focus on expanding your awareness outward: sounds, textures, colors, movements, temperature.

This strengthens sensory presence and dissolves mental chatter.

5. The Trigger Tracking Challenge

For three days, track every moment you feel irritated, anxious, defensive, or activated.
For each trigger, write:

- What happened
- What emotion appeared
- What belief it touched
- How your body reacted

This reveals deep subconscious patterns and opens the door to reprogramming.

6. The Higher Self Embodiment Hour

Choose one hour a day to fully embody your higher self.
During that hour, act, speak, respond, breathe, and think as the highest version of you would.

This trains your nervous system to normalize elevated behavior.

7. The Silence Challenge

Commit to one hour (or one morning) of intentional silence.
No talking, texting, or social media.
Use the time for observation instead of input.

This strengthens internal awareness and intuition.

8. The Presence-with-Others Challenge

Choose one person each day to give your full, undivided presence.
No multitasking. No anticipating their next words.
Just pure listening and awareness.

This deepens connection and mindful communication.

9. The Mindful Nourishment Reset

Choose one meal a day for a week to eat in complete mindfulness:
slowly, silently, with gratitude, and full sensory presence.
Notice emotions, cravings, and fullness cues.

This reconnects you to intuition and self-trust.

10. The Energy Audit Challenge

For one week, track how your energy shifts in different environments, conversations, and tasks.
Identify which ones drain you and which ones elevate you.
Choose one thing to release and one thing to expand.

This aligns your life with your higher self.

In many spiritual traditions, the third eye (known as *ajna* in Sanskrit) is the energy center associated with intuition, inner wisdom, and a deeper sense of awareness. Mindfulness, at its core, is the practice of bringing one's attention to the present moment without judgment. These two concepts are deeply intertwined because a mindful practice is often a key to awakening and balancing the third eye chakra. If you are not familiar with the third eye chakra, I have added a section at the end of the book where I go into a bit more detail about what chakras are and provide more information.

1. The Core Connection: Inner Awareness

- **Mindfulness as a Tool:** Mindfulness practices, particularly meditation, are a primary way to quiet the "monkey mind"—(a classic term used for centuries in Buddhist teachings) the constant stream of thoughts, worries, and plans that can obscure your intuition. By focusing on your breath or a specific point, you train your mind to become more still. This stillness is what allows you to access the deeper, more subtle insights associated with the third eye.
- **The Third Eye as the Goal:** The third eye is the seat of "inner vision" or "perception." A balanced third eye chakra allows you to see beyond the surface level of things, to understand underlying truths, and to trust your gut feelings. Mindfulness helps you cultivate the presence and non-attachment needed to receive and interpret this inner guidance. Within the book, I have added a section that further explains the third eye. Practical Ways to Tie Them Together

A. Meditation and Visualization

- **Focused-Point Meditation:** This is one of the most direct ways to connect the two. Find a quiet place to sit comfortably. Close your eyes and bring your attention to the space between your eyebrows. This is the location of the third eye chakra. As you breathe, simply focus your awareness on this point.

- **Light Visualization:** A powerful technique is to visualize a glowing, indigo or violet light at your third eye center. As you inhale, imagine this light becoming brighter and more vibrant. As you exhale, imagine it expanding and radiating a sense of clarity and peace throughout your entire head and body. This mindful visualization actively engages the third eye.
- **Mantra Chanting:** Chanting mantras like "Om" or "Aum" is believed to resonate with the third eye's vibrational frequency. You can mindfully repeat the mantra, focusing the sound and vibration on the area between your eyebrows.

B. Mindful Breathing (Pranayama)

- **Mindful Breathing Practices:** The breath is a fundamental anchor for mindfulness. By paying close attention to your inhale and exhale, you ground yourself in the present moment. This calm, focused state is essential for third eye work.
- **Alternate Nostril Breathing (Nadi Shodhana):** This specific breathing exercise is excellent for balancing the two hemispheres of the brain and calming the nervous system. This state of balance and tranquility is thought to be very conducive to awakening the third eye.

C. Body Awareness

- **Yoga Poses:** Certain yoga poses are said to stimulate the pineal gland, which is often linked to the third eye. Poses like Child's Pose (Balasana), Downward-Facing Dog (Adho Mukha Svanasana), or standing forward bends can be done with a mindful focus on the sensation in your forehead area.

- **Mindful Movement:** As you move through your daily life or a yoga sequence, bring your full attention to the physical sensations of your body. This practice of body-scan meditation helps to deepen your overall awareness, which is a key component of a balanced third eye chakra.

3. The Benefits of This Practice

By combining mindfulness with a focus on the third eye chakra,

you can experience several benefits:

- **Increased Intuition:** You may find it easier to trust your gut instincts and make decisions with a sense of inner knowing.
- **Greater Clarity:** The "mental fog" that often comes with an overactive or underactive mind can dissipate, leading to clearer thoughts and a better understanding of yourself and the world.
- **Enhanced Self-Awareness:** The practice encourages a deep introspection that helps you confront and understand your beliefs, motivations, and fears.
- **Reduced Stress and Anxiety:** The calm and focused state achieved through mindful practices can significantly reduce feelings of stress and anxiety.
- **Improved Creativity and Imagination:** An open and balanced third eye is associated with a boost in creativity and the ability to visualize your goals and desires

Throughout this book, mindfulness has been described as attention, awareness, and the ability to meet the present moment without judgment. One of the simplest ways to experience this kind of awareness is through a poetic form that requires us to slow down and observe with intention.

This form is called Haiku.The journey of self expression by finding inspiration, healing and personal transformation. Haiku, an ancient Japanese form of short, simple poetry, is appealing to so many due to it being short, expressive and therapeutic in nature. Haiku uses only 17 syllables and requires no writing skills. This can be a form of journaling. To help put it into perspective, here are some examples, keep in mind it does not have to be perfect.

Presence

Breath enters, breath leaves (5)
Nothing else is asked of me (7)
This moment is full (5)

Awareness

Morning light pauses
On the edge of quiet thought
I notice myself

Letting Go

Leaves release the branch
No lesson, no resistance
Just the art of fall

Emotional Regulation

A wave rises strong
I do not become the sea
I remain the shore

Acceptance

Clouds cross the blue sky
Never asking to remain
Neither do my thoughts

Grounding

Bare feet on the earth
The mind returns to the body
Here is where I stand

Mindful Choice

Before I respond
I meet the space in between
And choose gently now

Compassion (Self)

I place my hand here
Where the ache is asking me
To listen, not fix

Haiku can be used as a form of bullet journaling if you would want, you can get a plain notebook and use it for this form of mindfulness, as you are sitting in a park enjoying nature or any moments in your life.

Mindful Bullet Journaling

I am really excited to have included a bullet journal in the book for you and I hope you are just as excited to use this awesome tool.

In book one Journaling is good for our Mental Health, Bullet journaling was introduced. I want to discuss mindful bullet journaling with additional details here to ensure we are not leaving any stone unturned.

Mindful bullet journaling isn't about creating the prettiest spread or filling every page with tasks. It's about slowing down enough to notice the small details of your life as you write them. Each bullet becomes a reminder: to breathe, to reflect, to be fully present. It's a space where your to-do list meets your inner stillness."

Mindful bullet journaling combines both: it helps you track your days *while* anchoring yourself in the present moment.
Example: Instead of just writing "meeting at 2 PM," you might add a mindful note like, *"Take three deep breaths before entering."*

It's not about rigid rules or perfect pages. It's about using bullets, symbols, or short reflections to keep awareness alive.
Example: Symbols like:

🌿 = moments of gratitude
☀ = something that brought joy
🌀 = something that felt overwhelming

Taking the time to pause instead of rushing, let the journal become a daily "mini-meditation."

Example entry:
■ Finish report
Mindful tea break (pause, notice taste/aroma)
Notice the moon tonight

Traditional journaling captures thoughts and stories. Bullet journaling organizes tasks and goals. When I first added bullet journaling I had to have the bullet in front of every one line added into my journal.

I want to show you how simple this can be. Your bullet journal has about 30 questions. In the section that only has bullets you can add one word or a sentence.

The purpose is to share how this can be a quick journal entry of 60 seconds. Use the space below to add 5 of your favorite movies.

I have added space for you below to get started with bullet journaling.

Write down anything that resonates with you. There are no hard rules. 

*

*

*

*

Mindful Bullet Journal

"One word to describe my mood today is…"

"What did I notice about my breath today?"

"A simple joy I experienced was…"

What sensation in my body do I notice most right now?

If my mind had a weather forecast today, it would be…
What is one thing I did slowly and with intention today?
What's a gentle reminder I want to carry into tomorrow?
How can I create more space for stillness in my day?

Think of what you can do daily.

*

*

*

*

*

*

*

*

*

*

*

*

*

One word that describes how I feel right now is…

What is one small thing I can appreciate about today?

A sound I noticed today was…

How did my body feel this morning when I woke up?

What was a simple joy I experienced today?

One thing I am letting go of is…

One thing I am inviting in is…

How did I care for myself today?

What emotion visited me today?

Something in nature I noticed today was…

What made me smile today?

When did I feel most present today?

What is one kind thing I can do for myself tomorrow?

My breath feels like…

The color that captures my mood right now is…

What gave me energy today?

What drained my energy today?

How can I show myself compassion right now?

A small act of mindfulness I practiced today was…

What am I grateful for in this exact moment?

One thing I usually overlook but noticed today was…

What does stillness mean to me right now?

How did I connect with another person today?

What do I need less of in my life?

What do I need more of in my life?

60 SECOND MINDFUL BULLET JOURNAL 

*

*

*

*

*

*

*

*

*

*

*

Mindful Friendships

Relationships come in a variety of forms and Friendships are certainly a part of them. Mindful friendships are connections built on presence, honesty, compassion, and emotional awareness. They are not just people you enjoy — they are people you *grow with*, people you can be your full self around, and people who value the exchange of energy as much as the exchange of words.

In a world of rushed conversations, distracted connections, and surface-level interactions, mindful friendships remind us to slow down and feel the relationship. They invite us to check in — with ourselves and with each other — with intention. In those rare moments when life appears to be turning upside down it is nice to have a friend who cares, can offer advice and be there for emotional support. Friendship is a two way street.

What Makes a Friendship Mindful?

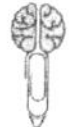

1. Presence

You're not just "there" together — you're truly with each other.
Listening without rushing. Sharing without competing.
Your attention becomes a gift.

2. Emotional Awareness

Mindful friends look beyond the surface and take note of feelings.
They ask, "How are you *really* doing?"
They notice shifts in tone, energy, and spirit without judgment.

3. Non-Attachment

Mindful friendships grow without pressure.
There's space to evolve.
No one clings, controls, or keeps score.
Support is offered freely, not demanded.

4. Respect for Boundaries

Healthy boundaries are honored, not punished.
Mindful friends understand that space, rest, and quiet are sometimes needed — and they don't take it personally.

5. Accountability With Compassion

A mindful friend can tell you the truth with love.
They hold you to your higher self, not your mistakes.

Why Mindful Friendships Matter

- They reduce stress and emotional overwhelm.
- They deepen your sense of belonging and safety.
- They help regulate your nervous system through co-regulation.
- They support mental health and resilience.
- They mirror back your worth, your growth, and your potential.

Mindful friendships nourish your spirit the same way mindful breathing nourishes your body. I am enjoying witnessing one of my sons actively participate in mindful friendships. He hosted a FriendsGiving in one of the local parks and it went well. All invited participated by contributing in some capacity to help make the event a success. I have also witnessed him plan weekend trips with friends, birthday celebrations and a day filled with games. He reminds me that this is an area that I must be intentional with and it is currently a work in progress.

I must add that my friends are just as busy in life as I am and when we speak on the phone it is for hours or when we see each other and spend time together it is for hours that we sit, eat, chat, laugh and plan our next get together. I have found that real friendships endure the test of time and do not require weekly or daily meetings to remain intact but mindful when we are in each other's presence.

We are not holding our cellphones in hand scrolling social media, we are not glaring at Tiktok videos for an hour. We are present.

How to Cultivate Mindfulness in Your Friendships

- **Practice being fully present when you're together.**
  Put the phone away. Listen deeply.
- **Communicate your needs and boundaries clearly.**
  Mindful friendships thrive on honesty.
- **Check in intentionally.**
  A simple "Thinking of you today" goes a long way.
- **Celebrate the wins.**
  Small victories matter.
- **Allow space for imperfection.**
  Mindful friendships are human, not flawless.
- **Reflect on the balance.**
  Ask yourself: Is the energy mutually supportive?

Reflection Prompt

"What qualities do I value most in my friendships, and how can I show up more mindfully for the people I care about?"

Mindful Coloring

Mindful coloring is more than filling in shapes—it's a gentle practice of slowing down, breathing deeply, and bringing awareness to each stroke of color. It invites calm into busy moments, fosters creativity, and helps restore balance to the mind and body.

"Every page is an opportunity to color your way back into existence."

I have created an Adult Mindfulness coloring line that assists with the following:

- Reduces Stress & Anxiety
- Encourages Presence & Focus
- Boosts Creativity & Self-Expression
- Improves Mood & Emotional Balance
- Enchances Mind-Body Connection
- Supports Sleep & Relaxation
- Easy, Non-intimidating and enjoyable for all ages

These coloring books are available on Amazon and also on my website. I have found that people enjoy adult coloring books as many of them realize the benefits. I also enjoy traveling to various events and setting up popup shops for those near to purchase the coloring books or any of my writings.

" The little things? The little moments? They aren't little."

-Jon Kabatt-Zinn

Mindful Coloring

Mandalas are ancient geometric designs known for their meditative qualities. In this activity, you'll have the opportunity to color a mandala mindfully, focusing on each stroke and your breath.

Find a comfortable quiet place to work. Gather your coloring materials, crayons, colored pens and colored pencils. Take a few deep breaths to center yourself and clear your mind.

1. Observe the intricate mandala design in front of you.

2. Take a moment to appreciate the patterns and details of the mandala.

3. Consider what colors you would like to use that resonate with you and trust your instincts.

Reduces Stress and Anxiety

Coloring helps calm the nervous system by focusing your attention on simple, repetitive motions. It activates the parasympathetic nervous system — the “rest and digest” mode — which naturally lowers stress levels. Take a moment to reflect on your experience.

Promotes Mindfulness and Presence

When you color mindfully, you focus on the colors, shapes, and movement of your hands. This anchors you in the present moment, gently quieting racing thoughts.

Enhances Emotional Regulation

Coloring can serve as a safe emotional outlet, helping you process feelings through color choices and the creative process. It's a soothing, nonverbal form of expression.

Improves Concentration
Mindful coloring strengthens your ability to focus. It trains your brain to sustain attention without judgment — a skill that translates to other mindfulness practices and daily life.

Stimulates Creativity

Choosing colors and blending shades taps into your intuitive, creative side. It awakens the right hemisphere of your brain — the part associated with imagination, intuition, and holistic thinking.

Exercising Mindfulness

Mindful Smelling Exercise

After Covid-19, I was informed by many that they lost the ability to smell, I empathize with them. If you are someone who cannot smell, no worries you may proceed to the next section, but keep in mind you can share this with a family member or a friend. If you are thinking "what is a mindful smelling exercise" you are not alone. I have been asked this question a few times by others who were aware that I was writing a book about mindfulness and as I shared various parts of the book this section raised a few eyebrows.

A **mindful smelling exercise** is the practice of using your sense of smell to anchor yourself in the present moment. It involves intentionally focusing your attention on a particular scent — noticing its layers, sensations, and the emotional or physical responses it evokes — without judgment or distraction.

You can do this with:

- Essential oils or incense
- A cup of tea or coffee
- Fresh flowers or herbs
- Food before eating
- Even the scent of rain, the ocean, or nature around you

It's about slowing down and fully *experiencing* the scent — allowing it to become a tool for grounding, awareness, and calm.

I want you to now take a few slow breaths with an essential oil such as Orange, or Lavender, or pick something pleasant or meaningful to you and simply notice:

Inhale deeply through the nose, exhale slowly through the mouth. Breathe in gently and observe what happens. Ask yourself the following questions.

* Where do I feel this in my body?

* What memory or feeling arises with this scent?

* How does my breath shift as I inhale it?

Mindfulness is often described as paying attention to the present through our breath, thoughts and body sensations. But one of the most powerful doorways into presence is our sense of smell. A familiar scent can transport us instantly, grounding us in the moment in a way that words often cannot. Essential oils offer us a simple, natural way to explore this practice. By pausing to notice the aroma of lavender, peppermint or any oil you are drawn towards, you create a mindful pause, an invitation to breathe deeper, feel calmer and awaken your senses. Essential oils are helpful in my household for my entire family.

Mindful Of Kindness

I live in sunny Arizona. We were on the news as the top state for road rage. This certainly concerns me, not in a way where it is keeping me up all night but, I realize we need mindfulness in this area, the road rules engagement reminder and this is one that we can certainly say "They should have taught this when we were kids " Kindness is the skill of being compassionate toward others, and when you practice mindful kindness, you stay present enough to recognize when kindness is needed—both for others and for yourself. Self-kindness is connected to happiness. It will help you to tend to your needs and help you with your approach to a negative thought. This is a part of our personal growth and connected to self love. Challenging unhelpful thinking and determining what things are in your control versus what is not. Adding in mindful kindness is an absolute in today's society.

Mindful Kindness to Yourself

- Speak to yourself with the same compassion you would offer a close friend.
- Pause and notice when you're being self-critical; gently reframe with kindness.
- Allow yourself rest without guilt when your body or mind asks for it.
- Celebrate small wins and progress, not just big achievements.
- Set healthy boundaries and honor your energy levels.
- Offer yourself forgiveness for past mistakes—release, don't relive.
- Practice mindful self-care (deep breaths, a cup of tea, a mindful walk, or journaling).
- Begin or end the day with an affirmation of self-worth.

Mindful Kindness to Others

- Practice deep listening—be fully present without planning your response.
- Offer a genuine smile or kind word, even to a stranger.
- Acknowledge someone's effort, not just their outcome.
- Extend patience when others are rushed, frustrated, or distracted.
- Offer help when you see a need, even in small ways.

- Express gratitude sincerely and often.
- Respect others' boundaries and honor their pace.
- Send a silent blessing or wish of well-being when someone comes to mind.

Take a moment to write down any thoughts that may have come to you as you were reading through mindful kindness. Do you practice mindful kindness with others? What about with yourself? Who is it that you need to practice mindful kindness with?

Mindful of Exploring Your Support System

It's not just listing "who's there for you." It's a process of *noticing* how you feel when you think about each person or connection, how energy flows between you, and whether those connections align with your well-being and growth.

It's also about recognizing that your support system isn't limited to people — it can include:

- Spiritual connections (your faith, ancestors, guides, nature)
- Emotional supports (journaling, therapy, art, meditation)
- Communal supports (friends, colleagues, mentors, online groups)
- Inner supports (your intuition, resilience, compassion for self)

Why it Matters:

Mindfulness grows stronger when we feel supported. Just as plants thrive with sunlight, water and good soil, we thrive when our environment and relationships nurture presence, peace and growth. A mindful support system helps us return to balance when life feels overwhelming.

Elements of a Mindful Support System

Supportive people

Surround yourself with friends, family, or mentors who encourage calm, compassion, and authentic living.

Seek out people who listen deeply, honor your boundaries, and remind you of your values.

Consider joining a mindfulness group, meditation circle, or journaling community.

Supportive spaces

Create a physical environment that brings you peace—a cozy corner, a nature spot, or a clutter-free desk.

Use calming cues like soft lighting, plants, essential oils, or gentle music to signal "this is my mindful space."

Supportive practices

Build daily rituals that ground you—morning breathing, mindful journaling, evening gratitude reflection.

Keep a "mindful check-in" habit: pause for 1–2 minutes throughout the day to notice your breath and body.

Supportive Tools

Journals, mindful coloring books, guided meditations, or apps can help keep you on track.
A simple object (stone, bracelet, photo, mantra card) can serve as a tangible reminder to return to presence.

Supportive Self-Talk

Speaking to yourself with the same kindness, understanding, and encouragement that you would offer a close friend.

It's the *inner dialogue* that uplifts, reassures, and guides you through challenges — instead of criticizing, doubting, or shaming you. Supportive self-talk helps you build a more compassionate relationship with yourself and strengthens your emotional well-being.

It's not about pretending everything is perfect — it's about meeting yourself where you are, with empathy and truth. Treat yourself with kindness, especially in difficult moments.

Instead of saying:

> "I messed up again. I'll never get this right."
> Try:
> "I'm still learning. It's okay to make mistakes — they help me grow."

Instead of:

> "I'm not good enough for this."
> Try:
> "I may not have all the answers yet, but I have the ability to learn and improve."

Instead of:

> "I can't handle this."
> Try:
> "This is tough, but I've handled difficult things before. I can take it one step at a time."

Replace “I should” or “I failed” with words of encouragement: *“I am learning, I am growing, I am enough.”*

Supportive self-talk is **self-kindness in action** — a mindful dialogue that nurtures growth rather than judgment.

It reminds you that your words (even the silent ones) carry energy, and you have the power to make that energy healing, encouraging, and full of love.

Mindful “self-talk” is necessary. It will then project outward towards others. We become what we practice most often.

Mindful Healthy Living

Noticing how certain foods make your body feel is a mindful practice in itself.

Asking yourself "How does my body feel when I choose whole, nourishing foods?" We have already talked about mindful eating and slowing down to notice the flavors, textures and how the food affects our energy.

Mindful supplementing is when you pause before adding something new, noticing its impacts over time. Let's discuss Holistic support, your body is your greatest teacher, notice how different foods and natural remedies make you feel. This section could be a stand alone book, while I am sharing a handful of healthy living tips as it relates to mindfulness there is so much more you can research and study. The following are some of the items our family uses to practice healthy living.

Mindful Hydration

Instead of just "drink more water," try:

- Drink a glass of water *before* checking your phone in the morning.
- Pause before each sip and notice temperature, texture, and how your body feels.

This supports digestion, energy, and cellular function.

Sea Moss

Sea Moss is often praised for minerals, digestion, and immune support. There are plenty of benefits. If you can get past the smell of some of these you will gain the following.

Rich in Essential Nutrients

Sea moss contains *over 90 minerals* that the body needs, including iodine, zinc, calcium, magnesium, potassium, iron, and vitamins A, C, E, K, and B complex. It helps fill nutritional gaps in the diet naturally.

Supports Thyroid Health
Because it's high in **iodine**, sea moss helps regulate thyroid function — which is essential for metabolism, energy, and hormone balance.

Boosts Immunity
Its antimicrobial and antiviral properties, along with antioxidants and vitamin C, help strengthen the immune system and protect against illness.

Aids Digestion
Sea moss is rich in **prebiotic fiber**, which nourishes gut bacteria and supports healthy digestion. It also soothes the digestive tract and may help relieve bloating and acid reflux.

Promotes Healthy Skin, Hair, and Nails
Its collagen-supporting minerals and hydration properties promote skin elasticity, hair growth, and a natural glow from within. Many people use it topically in masks as well.

Improves Joint and Bone Health
Sea moss contains omega-3 fatty acids, magnesium, and calcium — all of which help reduce inflammation and support bone strength and mobility.

Boosts Energy and Endurance
Its high iron and potassium content help oxygenate the blood, improve energy levels, and support mental focus.

Supports Weight Management
The fiber in sea moss helps you feel full longer and supports metabolism and natural detoxification.

Essential Oils

(internal use with guidance) – lemon for cleansing, peppermint for digestion, etc. I make my own essential oils and also offer them for sale to the public. My entire family enjoys the benefits.

Boost Immunity: Oils like eucalyptus, tea tree, and oregano have antiviral and antibacterial properties that help protect the body from illness.

Relieve Pain and Inflammation: Peppermint, lavender, and frankincense can ease tension, headaches, and sore muscles.

Improve Sleep: Lavender, chamomile, and cedarwood help relax the body and promote deep, restorative rest.

Support Respiratory Health: Eucalyptus, rosemary, and peppermint open airways and support easier breathing.

Aid Digestion: Ginger, peppermint, and fennel oils soothe digestive discomfort and nausea.

Balance Hormones: Clary sage, geranium, and ylang-ylang can help stabilize mood swings and menstrual symptoms.

Reduce Stress & Anxiety: Lavender, bergamot, and ylang-ylang calm the nervous system.

Enhance Focus & Clarity: Lemon, peppermint, and rosemary help sharpen mental alertness.

Lift Mood & Combat Fatigue: Citrus oils like orange, grapefruit, and lime energize and elevate your spirits.

Encourage Mindfulness: Frankincense, sandalwood, and patchouli deepen meditation and grounding practices.

Ease Emotional Release: Rose, clary sage, and chamomile support processing grief, sadness, and overwhelm.

Grounding: Vetiver, patchouli, and cedarwood connect you to the Root Chakra, providing stability and calm.

Heart Opening: Rose, geranium, and jasmine open the Heart Chakra for love, compassion, and forgiveness.

Intuition & Clarity: Frankincense, lavender, and sandalwood support the Third Eye Chakra, enhancing insight and awareness.

Purification & Protection: Sage, palo santo, and lemon cleanse energy fields and clear stagnant vibrations.

Manifestation & Creativity: Orange, cinnamon, and bergamot stimulate the Solar Plexus and Sacral Chakras, encouraging confidence and creative flow.

Herbal Teas

Chamomile for calm, Ginger for warmth, Green tea for energy.

Boosts Immunity: Teas like echinacea, elderberry, and ginger strengthen the immune system and help the body fight off infections.
Aids Digestion: Peppermint, ginger, and chamomile soothe the stomach, ease bloating, and support gut health.
Reduces Inflammation: Turmeric, rooibos, and green tea contain powerful anti-inflammatory compounds that support joint and tissue health.
Promotes Restful Sleep: Chamomile, lavender, and valerian root calm the nervous system and prepare the body for deep rest.
Supports Detoxification: Dandelion root, burdock, and nettle tea help cleanse the liver and flush toxins naturally.
Balances Hormones: Red raspberry leaf, spearmint, and chasteberry teas support reproductive health and hormonal balance.

Hydrates the Body: Herbal teas are a delicious way to stay hydrated while gaining additional nutritional benefits.
Reduces Stress and Anxiety: Lemon balm, chamomile, and passionflower soothe overactive thoughts and calm the heart.
Enhances Focus and Clarity: Ginkgo biloba, rosemary, and green tea gently sharpen mental alertness and memory.
Encourages Emotional Balance: Rose, lavender, and hibiscus promote feelings of peace, love, and openness.
Supports Mindfulness Practices: The act of brewing, smelling, and slowly sipping tea naturally invites you into the present moment — it becomes meditation in motion.

Use **organic herbs** when possible to avoid pesticides.
Consult with your healthcare provider if you're pregnant, nursing, or on medications. Some herbs are potent — always research proper dosages and combinations.

MINDFULLIVING

Black Seed Oil

Immune Support - Black seed oil contains thymoquinone, an antioxidant compound that may help support the body's natural immune defenses by reducing oxidative stress.

Anti-Inflammatory Properties - Many people use it because it may help ease everyday inflammation and support joint comfort.

Skin + Hair Health - Used topically for:

- Hydrating dry skin
- Supporting clearer skin
- Soothing minor irritation
- Promoting softer, stronger hair and scalp health

Antioxidant Support

Its naturally occurring antioxidants can help protect cells from everyday wear caused by stress and environmental factors.

Digestive Comfort

Traditionally, black seed oil has been used to support:

- Bloating relief
- Mild gas reduction
- General digestive comfort

Support for Healthy Metabolism

Some early research suggests it may help support:

- Normal blood sugar levels (in people who already have healthy levels)
- A balanced metabolic response

Burdock Root

Rich in Antioxidants - Burdock root contains quercetin, luteolin, and phenolic acids, which help protect cells from oxidative stress.

Natural Detox Support - Traditionally, burdock has been used to support:

- Liver health
- Kidney function

It's often included in detox teas for this reason.

Skin Health - Burdock may help support clearer skin thanks to its:

- Anti-inflammatory properties
- Antibacterial effects

People often use it for skin conditions like dryness, irritation, or breakouts.

Digestive Support - It's high in inulin, a prebiotic fiber that helps:

- Improve digestion
- Support gut bacteria
- Promote smoother bowel movements

Blood Sugar Support - Because of its inulin content, burdock may help the body maintain more stable blood sugar levels (in people who already have normal levels).

Anti-Inflammatory Effects - Burdock is used to help ease general body inflammation and support joint comfort.

Circulation and Blood Purification (Traditional Use)

In traditional herbal medicine, burdock is considered a "blood purifier," helping support:

- Healthy circulation
- Removal of natural bodily wastes

Whole Foods – fresh fruits, vegetables, grains, nuts, and legumes are foods in their natural state, rich in nutrients and free from heavy processing.

"Mindfulness invites us to pay attention not only to our thoughts but also to what we place into our bodies. Each meal, sip of tea, or natural remedy is an opportunity to listen inwardly.

Asking yourself questions such as; Do I feel energized, calm, heavy, or clear?

This awareness is the foundation of mindful healthy living. Exploring holistic supports like sea moss, herbal teas, or essential oils can become an extension of mindfulness—tuning in to the body's wisdom as it responds. There are many benefits you can gain with adding mindfulness into this area of your life with whole foods.

Nourish the body with essential vitamins, minerals, and antioxidants.
Support digestion with natural fiber that promotes gut health.
Boost energy by providing clean, sustained fuel.
Balance mood through steady blood sugar and nutrient-rich meals.
Strengthen immunity with plant-based compounds that protect the body.
Encourage mindfulness by helping you slow down, taste, and connect with your food intentionally.

Gut-friendly foods include:

- Berries
- Citrus
- Leafy greens
- Garlic
- Ginger
- Fermented foods (yogurt, kimchi, sauerkraut)

Today, many people have realized the benefits of fasting. Fasting *mindfully* is very different from just "skipping meals." It's about **intention, awareness, and listening to your body**. I'll walk through the main benefits in a clear way and also call out where mindfulness really matters. Before getting started with fasting, I recommend you do additional research. I would not suggest you start out with a two day fast but work your way up to this if this is something you are interested in doing. Please, please do your research and seek professional assistance from a health professional or a certified health coach.

Better Relationship With Food (Less Emotional Eating)

Mindful fasting helps you:

- Notice **true hunger vs. habit or boredom**
- See how often you eat to soothe emotions (stress, loneliness, anxiety)
- Slow down and actually *taste* and appreciate your food when you do eat

Over time, this can:

- Reduce impulsive snacking
- Help you feel **more in control** rather than controlled by cravings
- Build gratitude for food instead of guilt or shame around it

Increased Mental Clarity & Focus

When done safely, many people report:

- Fewer energy crashes
- A lighter, clearer feeling in the mind
- More focus for work, creativity, or spiritual practices

Mindfulness boosts this effect because you're:

- Checking in with your body regularly
- Not overloading your system with constant grazing
- Using breathing and awareness instead of sugar/caffeine boosts

Nervous System & Stress Benefits

Mindful fasting invites you to:

- Sit with mild discomfort (like light hunger) without panicking
- Use breath and presence instead of reacting automatically

This can:

- Build **emotional resilience**
- Reduce stress-driven eating patterns
- Help you respond, not react, to body sensations

Pairing fasting with:

- Slow breathing
- Gentle stretching
- Journaling about what comes up emotionally

...can turn it into a powerful self-awareness practice.

Supporting Metabolic Health (General, Non-Medical Sense)

Without getting too technical, mindful fasting (like time-restricted eating) may help:

- Give your digestion a break between meals
- Support more stable energy rather than constant spikes and crashes
- Encourage more **intentional meal timing** (like not eating late out of habit)

The mindful part matters because:

- You're not white-knuckling through starvation
- You're choosing windows that feel sustainable and respectful to your body
- You're *listening*—if you feel dizzy, weak, or unwell, you adjust instead of forcing it

(Anything medical like diabetes, pregnancy, eating disorders, or specific conditions = always talk with a healthcare professional before fasting.)

Supporting the Body's Natural "Clean-Up" Processes

When you're not constantly digesting, your body has more space for:

- Repair and maintenance
- Balancing internal systems

Mindfulness supports this by:

- Reducing stress (which can interfere with repair)
- Encouraging deep rest and gentler activity on fasting days

Spiritual & Emotional Benefits

Mindful fasting is often used as:

- A way to reconnect with purpose or faith (in a non-dogmatic way)
- A reset from overconsumption and overstimulation
- A practice in **gratitude**, patience, and humility

Emotionally, it can:

- Bring buried feelings to the surface (which you can then process, not avoid)
- Help you see how often you use food to numb feelings

Stronger Body Awareness

Mindful fasting teaches you to recognize:

- What *true* hunger feels like vs. a craving
- Which foods make you feel energized vs. sluggish when you break the fast
- The difference between "I'm tired," "I'm stressed," and "I'm hungry"

That awareness can help with:

- More aligned food choices
- Better timing of meals
- More compassion toward your own body signals

How to Fast Mindfully (Not Harshly)

A few principles so it stays healthy & kind:

- **Start small**
  For example:
    - Stop eating 2–3 hours before bed
    - Or gently try a 12-hour overnight fast (like 7 pm to 7 am)
- **Stay present**
    - Check in: "What am I feeling in my body right now?"
    - Use slow breathing when hunger rises instead of panicking
- **Break the fast gently**

    - Eat slowly
    - Choose nourishing foods (not "reward binge" foods)
    - Notice how you feel before, during, and after

- **Respect your body's "no"**

    - If you feel dizzy, weak, shaky, or unwell → stop the fast and eat.
    - Mindfulness includes **self-protection**, not self-punishment.

Mindful Holistic Self-Love

"I think I love myself, I know I love myself." I am mindful when it comes to loving me. There are times where my heart gets this warm and fuzzy feeling as I send love energy to myself. This was something I did not think of frequently.

I no longer feel it is necessary to respond to the "self love is selfish and putting others before self is just how it has always been." I no longer feel this sense of guilt or embarrassment as if I must put myself last to fit in with those who are not aware that love starts with self and then expands out to others.

I am not speaking of becoming so self indulged that you cannot see, hear or feel the presence of others. Have you heard of the self love club? When I first heard of the self love club, I thought it was about a group of people who showed up in support of loving themselves and that they would share stories with one another, have special membership dues, adding another bill if I elected to join.

The Self-Love Club isn't a place with membership dues or secret handshakes — it's a state of being. It's the moment you speak kindly to yourself instead of criticizing. It's taking a deep breath before reacting. It's saying "no" when your peace says "yes, please." Joining the club means you commit to showing up for yourself every single day — flaws, fears, and all.

Holistic self-love is a concept that views self-love as more than just mental affirmations or positive thinking. It's about nurturing the whole self; body, mind, emotions and spirit. In other words, its self-love in action, awareness and care across all areas of life.

Components of Holistic Self-Love

1. **Body Care**
   - Nourishing your body with healthy foods, water, and supplements.
   - Moving your body in ways that feel joyful, not punishing. Resting when needed and honoring physical limits.

2. **Mind Care**
   - Practicing mindfulness, journaling, meditation, or reflection.
   - Challenging negative self-talk and nurturing a kind inner voice.
   - Learning and growing with curiosity rather than judgment.

3. **Emotional Care**
   - Feeling and processing emotions without suppression.
   - Seeking support when needed (friends, therapy, or support groups).
   - Practicing gratitude, forgiveness, and compassion—toward self and others.

4. **Spiritual Care**
   - Connecting with a sense of purpose or meaning.
   - Exploring meditation, prayer, or rituals that feel authentic.
   - Aligning actions with your values and inner guidance.

5. **Environmental & Relational Care**
   - Surrounding yourself with positive, supportive people.
   - Creating spaces that nourish calm, creativity, and inspiration.
   - Limiting exposure to negativity or toxicity in relationships or media.

Holistic self-love isn't just saying 'I love myself' in the mirror—it's about choosing practices, environments, foods, and thoughts that honor every part of you. It's a daily commitment to nurturing your body, mind, heart, and soul. When we practice self-love holistically, we cultivate a foundation of balance, resilience, and presence that naturally radiates into every part of our lives."

Combining Mindfulness and Holistic Self-Love

Combining mindfulness with holistic self-love shifts the focus from just practicing self-care to practicing with full awareness and presence. It's about being intentional and fully present in loving yourself in all areas.

Mindful Holistic Self-Love

Definition:
Mindful holistic self-love is the **intentional awareness of caring for your whole self**—body, mind, emotions, and spirit—in every moment. It's not just doing loving acts; it's **feeling, noticing, and fully engaging** with those acts of self-love.

How It Differs from Standard Holistic Self-Love

Standard Holistic Self-Love	**Mindful Holistic Self-Love**
Focuses on actions (eating healthy, exercising, meditating, affirming)	Focuses on *awareness of those actions*—noticing sensations, thoughts, and feelings as you do them
Standard Holistic Self-Love	**Mindful Holistic Self-Love**
Can sometimes become routine or mechanical	Encourages presence and deep engagement with each self-care act

Emphasizes outcomes (wellness, peace, balance)	Emphasizes the process and the *experience* of caring for yourself
Might overlook the small daily moments	Recognizes micro-moments of self-love (breath, gentle touch, mindful pauses)

Practical Ways to Practice Mindful Holistic Self-Love

1. **Mindful Eating:** Notice flavors, textures, and how the food nourishes your body.

2. **Mindful Movement:** Feel each stretch, step, or breath during exercise or walking.

3. **Mindful Reflection:** Journal or meditate while fully observing your thoughts and emotions without judgment.

4. **Mindful Breathing:** Pause to check in with your body and emotions throughout the day.

5. **Mindful Rituals:** Lighting a candle, drinking tea, or using essential oils with full awareness of the sensations, scents, and feelings they evoke.

6. **Mindful Gratitude & Compassion:** Actively feel gratitude and compassion for yourself and others, noticing the ripple effect in your body and mood.

Mirror Intention Ritual

Stand in front of a mirror, look into your own eyes, and speak one loving affirmation.
Not ten. Just one — slowly, intentionally.

This builds a relationship with your reflection rather than avoiding it.

Mindful Bath or Shower Ritual

While bathing, imagine the water washing away judgment, doubt, and heaviness.
Infuse the moment with gratitude: *"I deserve to feel cleansed, lighter, and renewed."*

This turns a daily routine into a healing moment.

A "Yes to Me" Commitment

Choose one small thing each day that is *just for you* — a boundary, a break, a meal, a quiet moment, or saying "no." Honor it as a self-love practice, not an indulgence.

This builds consistency in honoring your needs.

"Let yourself be silently drawn by the strange pull of what you really love. It will not lead you astray" ***- Rumi***

Mindfulness & Financial Well-Being

Mindfulness and Money, Creating Peace in Your Finances

Money is about energy, emotions and awareness and not just about numbers. When we bring mindfulness into how we earn, spend, and save, we begin to see that our financial life reflects our inner world. The more grounded and intentional we are, the more harmony we create, both in our household and within ourselves. Within my own immediate family, my husband and I had to be intentional with developing a money mindset over the years. Growing up there were years where we lacked the basic needs. My mother would stand in line to receive cheese, milk and beans.

There were many factors that played a role. Upon her relocating into a larger city where it was more about your skills and intellect vs your outer appearance money flowed frequently but was mismanaged. We found ourselves in the same situations, falling short of having the full rent, falling short of having food, falling short of having enough. Upon becoming an adult, I often over spent on my kids' clothing. I quickly learned to use lay-a-ways. Due to the lack of basic needs growing up, I found myself slightly more stable in the area of money. This simply means, I paid my bills, purchased food and had no money left, instead of taking trips, going out to restaurants, partying or buying fancy clothing. After having to live that way for years, I had developed a scarcity mindset and had to reprogram my relationship with money and develop a money mindset. Leaning into an abundance mindset.

Why it matters:

Money can be a source of stress, freedom, or both — and how we manage it greatly impacts the quality of our lives. Mindful spending isn't about restriction or deprivation; it's about *awareness and intention*. It's about noticing where your money goes, what values it supports, and how it affects your well-being.

I know firsthand how stressful it can be when funds are tight. There were times when I worried about where the next meal would come from, whether the lights would stay on, or how my then single mother would be able to afford to take care of us as kids.

Making choices between bills, food, and essentials is exhausting — both mentally and emotionally.

During challenging times, like the COVID-19 pandemic, which now feels so long ago, I found myself working multiple jobs — a full-time job, a part-time position, weekend work, and building my coaching business. I quickly realized that working so much was not sustainable for me. I learned that while financial pressure is inevitable for many, the way we approach spending and earning can make a difference. Mindfulness in this area isn't just about tracking dollars; it's about understanding your relationship with money, reducing stress, and creating space to make empowered choices. I was aware of mindful spending but was not mindful about spending.

Mindful spending helps you:

- Prioritize what truly matters — instead of reacting to impulse or societal pressures.
- Reduce anxiety and guilt — by making conscious choices aligned with your values.
- Create space for joy and growth — freeing up resources, time, and energy for what enriches your life.
- Build resilience for the future — giving you clarity and control even when money is tight.

One day I had my remote in my hand restlessly changing from one channel to the next. I landed on a program about Lottery winners and where they were after having won millions.

Do you know how many stories are out there of someone winning the lottery, thinking it's the miracle that'll fix everything — only to have their life blow up anyway. It's not just a few bad apples: studies estimate that **around 70% of lottery winners** will end up broke within five years of their win. Other analyses show **about 12% declare bankruptcy** within seven years, and many more face serious financial, relational or emotional fallout. Why? Because having money doesn't automatically give you the tools to manage it — to decide *how* you spend it, what you let in, what values you support, what lifestyle you build. It's a powerful warning: **wealth without awareness can become ruin**, not relief.

Contrast this with people who practice mindful spending — who treat money not just as “how much can I spend” but “does this dollar support the life I truly want?” Here’s where someone like Oprah offers an important perspective. She’s said that her focus “has never, ever for one minute been money,” but on purpose, meaning and alignment. And she offers a simple but profound question: “Will this fit into what I already have? Am I just caught up in the moment or is this of real use to me?”

So, what happens if you *don’t* bring mindfulness into your spending and financial decisions?

- You may chase illusions that money will solve everything — but end up carrying the same stress, or more.
- You may buy what society says you should, not what you truly value — so the happiness lease expires fast.
- You may skip the pause — the “Does this align?” moment — and wake up years later wondering where it all went.
- And when income drops, when job markets shift, when life throws curveballs (and it does) — lack of intentional spending leaves you vulnerable.

On the other hand, embedding mindfulness into how you earn, manage and spend money means you’re not just reacting — you’re choosing. You’re building a financial life that supports your core roles (coach, mother, wife, creator are a few of mine), not one that distracts or drains you. You’re less likely to be swept away by the “easy-wealth illusion” and more likely to stay grounded when windfalls or stresses come.

Mindfulness helps you notice your spending habits, reduce impulsive decisions, and align your financial choices with your values. It brings clarity, reduces money-related stress, and fosters a sense of control and gratitude. While, at first it might be difficult to follow this process for many who are impulsive spenders, you will find it to be helpful when you are in a financial crunch situation. Upon forming a habit of implementing mindfulness financial well-being it will become a way of life for you just like blinking, you do not have to say to your eyes blink, blink, blink that process is naturally built in.

Ways Mindfulness Can Show Up in Daily Finances

- **Conscious Spending**
    - Pause before each purchase: *Do I truly need this, or am I reacting emotionally?*
    - Notice the feelings or triggers behind spending—stress, boredom, or social pressure.
- **Budget Awareness**
    - Track expenses mindfully, not just mechanically. Observe patterns, without judgment.
    - Celebrate small financial wins as a form of positive reinforcement.
- **Mindful Saving & Investing**
    - Set intentions for your savings and investments. *Where do I want my money to support me and my life goals?*
    - Notice your emotional response when saving—gratitude, relief, or fear—and reflect on it.

- **Reducing Money Stress**
    - Use mindful breathing or short meditations when facing financial decisions or bills.
    - Recognize worry as a thought, not a reality—then plan action from clarity rather than panic.
- **Aligning Spending With Values**
    - Reflect: *Does this purchase or investment align with my values and long-term well-being?*
    - Mindfulness helps avoid "keeping up with others" or impulse buys, creating financial freedom rooted in purpose.
- **Gratitude for Resources**
    - Notice and appreciate what you *already* have. Gratitude can shift your mindset from scarcity to abundance.
- **Mindful Giving**
    - Whether it's time, money, or energy, give intentionally and notice the joy or fulfillment it brings.

Mindfulness isn't just for meditation cushions—it can guide every dollar, every choice, and every financial habit.

By bringing awareness to our spending, saving, and giving, we cultivate a sense of control, reduce stress, and align our resources with what truly matters. Mindful finances aren't about restriction—they're about conscious, compassionate decisions that support our well-being and long-term goals.

Mindful Money Exercise

Purpose: Bring awareness, intention, and calm to your financial habits while aligning spending, saving, and giving with your values.

1. Pause & Center

Take 3 deep breaths. Notice your body and your mind.
Prompt: "How do I feel when I think about my finances right now?"

____

____

2. Reflect on Spending

- What did I spend money on this week/month?

  ____

  ____

- Which purchases brought me joy or fulfillment?

  ____

- Which purchases felt impulsive or regretful?

  ____

  ____

- *Optional:* Circle or highlight spending that aligns with your values.

3. Saving & Goals Check-In

- What am I saving for right now (short-term or long-term)?

  ____

- How does saving make me feel—safe, restricted, proud?

  ____

- What small step can I take this week to support my savings goals?

  ____

4. Align With Your Values

- What matters most to me in life (health, family, experiences, security, growth)?

- Are my spending and saving choices aligned with these values?

  ____

- *Prompt:* Write one action you can take to better align your finances with your values.

  ____

5. Gratitude & Generosity

- List 1–3 things you are grateful for regarding your money/resources.

- Note any intentional giving you practiced or plan to practice (time, money, energy).

---

6. Mindful Money Intention

Prompt: Write a short intention for your financial well-being this week/month.
Example: "I will spend and save with awareness, patience, and alignment with my values." you may need to use a notebook.

In the past I have had a handful of guests on my podcast that wrote books about finances and who shared plenty of tips and tools. I have spoken with Multi-Millionaires who shared so much when the show stopped recording. I nearly studied these folks and had so many questions for them. One thing that surprised me the most was that they were "Mindful" in many areas and this included kindness.

They were nothing like what most people perceive people with an unusual amount of money to be. Many have a belief that people with money are greedy, evil, rude, cruel, ruthless, or anything that is not positive. Having the opportunity to sit with so many and talk hours upon hours has been invaluable. I often sit quietly, actively listening and realize there is so much value I can add into many of the spaces I frequent. I attempt to share in small doses giving small nuggets of knowledge when moved to do so.

Songs About Mindfulness, Presence and Awareness

Music is one of my loves. I had to do a little research to find songs that are about mindfulness. I thought this would be a fun section to add in the book and a plus for those who enjoy listening to music.

Songs about mindfulness are not just a playlist of music, they are invitations to pause, breathe and be present.

Pop / Contemporary: Listen to the lyrics. You can also create your own list of songs that remind you of mindfulness. Keep any songs from this list that you like.

1. **"Let It Be" – The Beatles (acceptance, surrender)**
2. Breathe (2 AM)" – Anna Nalick (pause, awareness in struggle)
3. "Here Comes the Sun" – The Beatles (hope, new beginnings)
4. "Count on Me" – Bruno Mars (presence in friendship/support)
5. "Banana Pancakes" – Jack Johnson (slowing down, being present)
6. "Holocene" – Bon Iver (self-awareness and perspective)
7. . **"Don't Worry Be Happy" – Bobby McFerrin** (lighthearted presence)
8. . "Slow Down" – India.Arie (literally about slowing life's pace)

   Spiritual / Uplifting
9. **"Three Little Birds" – Bob Marley** (presence, letting go of worry)
10. **"One Day" – Matisyahu** (hopeful mindfulness for a better world)
11. **"Om Namo" – Deva Premal (mantra meditation in music form)**
12. **"Saturn" – Sleeping at Last (awareness of time and wonder)**

13. **"Weightless" – Marconi Union (scientifically shown to reduce stress & induce calm)**

Instrumental / Sound Healing

14. **"Weightless" – Marconi Union (proven relaxing effect)**
15. "Clair de Lune" – Claude Debussy (gentle presence)
16. Tibetan Singing Bowl recordings (deep meditative focus)
17. **Crystal Singing Bowl meditation tracks (healing vibrations)**
18. **"Ambient 1: Music for Airports" – Brian Eno (mindful ambient music)**

Best U.S. National Parks for Mindful Practice

I enjoy visiting parks and find them to be so relaxing. Living in Arizona, we can drive a few hours in each direction and land in an area of nature that is breathtaking. In this section of the book, I have added the best U.S National parks in the event you are in the area you can always implement the practice of mindfulness.

Mindfulness in national parks transforms ordinary moments into meditative experiences. Whether you're tracing ancient cliffs, listening to wind through redwoods, or pacing atop silent dunes, these landscapes open us to presence, perspective, and peace.

These parks are not just places to visit—they are invitations to *be*."

1. Olympic National Park (Washington)

Listening to Silence

With its moss-draped rainforests, wild coastline, and alpine vistas, Olympic offers diverse quiet havens. In the Hoh Rainforest lies the famed "One Square Inch of Silence"—widely regarded as one of the quietest spots in the U.S., perfect for deeply mindful listening.

- **Practice:** Find a quiet spot in the Hoh Rainforest. Sit or stand still. Close your eyes and tune into the layers of sound—the rustle of leaves, distant bird calls, drops of water. Each time your mind wanders, gently return to the soundscape.

- **Intention:** Awaken deep listening and appreciation for natural stillness.

2. Grand Canyon National Park (Arizona)

Expansive Breathwork

The vastness and ancient geology of the Grand Canyon naturally cultivate presence. Whether you're watching the sunrise along the rim or descending the Bright Angel Trail, this landscape awakens awe, perspective, and inner stillness

Practice: Stand at the rim, feet firmly grounded. Inhale deeply, imagining you're drawing in the vastness of the canyon. Exhale slowly, letting go of what feels heavy or small. Repeat for 5–7

breaths.
Intention: Anchor awe and perspective into the breath.

3. Acadia National Park (Maine)

Ocean Flow Walking

With rugged coastline, misty forest, and Cadillac Mountain sunrise views, Acadia is deeply grounding. The expansive ocean and quiet forest scenes invite awe and introspection.

Practice: Walk along the rocky coastline, syncing each step with the rhythm of the waves. With every inhale, step forward; with every exhale, release into the stride.

Intention: Align inner rhythm with the ocean's timeless pulse.

4. Glacier National Park (Montana)

Sky-Gazing Meditation

Remote, pristine, and serene—Glacier's glacial lakes, towering peaks, and dark night skies are ideal for solo reflection and silent stargazing.

Practice: At a lake or clearing, lie back and gaze at the sky or stars. Notice the vastness without labeling clouds, colors, or constellations. Allow thoughts to drift like passing clouds.
Intention: Cultivate spacious awareness and trust in the flow of time.

5. Zion National Park (Utah)

Grounding with Stone

Zion's dramatic canyons and the gentle flow of the Virgin River offer both exhilarating hikes and peaceful pockets. The Narrows and slot canyons encourage focused presence and embodied awareness.

Practice: Place your hands on a warm rock face or canyon wall. Feel its texture, warmth, and stillness. Take slow breaths, drawing stability and strength from the ancient stone.
Intention: Ground body and spirit through connection with earth's endurance.

6. Great Sand Dunes National Park (Colorado)

Walking Meditation on Sand

Walking atop Star Dune—North America's tallest dune—opens up expansive silence and stillness. The wide-open landscape invites walking meditation and inner calm

Practice: Walk barefoot on the dunes. Notice how your feet sink, how balance shifts, and how each step requires attention. Move slowly, pausing often.

Intention: Embrace impermanence and mindful balance.

7. Canyonlands National Park (Utah)

Silent Horizon Practice

Far less crowded than nearby parks, Canyonlands offers solitude among sweeping canyons, mesas, and desert silence—especially in its remote backcountry regions

Practice: Sit facing the horizon. Allow your gaze to soften, taking in the vast expanse without focusing on a single point. Breathe with openness.

Intention: Invite stillness and clarity by mirroring the desert's wide silence.

8. Redwood National and State Parks (California)

Tree Connection

Towering redwoods, filtered morning fog, and cathedral-like groves create an atmosphere of sanctuary—perfect for grounding, deep breaths, and forest bathing.

Practice: Stand with your back against a redwood. Feel its enormity, notice your breath aligning with its rooted presence. Imagine exhaling what you no longer need into the soil, inhaling strength from its towering form.
Intention: Root deeply and expand into grounded presence.

9. Isle Royale National Park (Michigan)

Canoe Reflection

Accessible only by boat or seaplane, Isle Royale is a remote island wilderness with minimal human presence. Paddle, hike, and move mindfully in this truly immersive natural setting.

Practice: While paddling, pause to let the canoe float. Close your eyes and feel the water rocking beneath you. Breathe with its rhythm. Let the water hold you fully.

Intention: Surrender into flow and trust the support of nature.

10. Boundary Waters Canoe Area Wilderness (Minnesota)

Twilight Mindfulness

Paddling through quiet lakes and forested canoe routes, especially at dusk, this place infuses peaceful solitude and attuned awareness—perfect for contemplative journeying.

Practice: As dusk falls, sit by the water. Notice the shift in light, sound, and temperature. Breathe with the transition, letting day dissolve into night.

Intention: Attune to cycles of change and the calm of endings and beginnings.

Why These Parks

Upon becoming a young adult all of the reasons listed below were the main reasons why I had a sort of love, yet hate relationship with parks, unless I was with my kids. I found these things to be less exciting than attending a comedy club or a Karaoke hot spot. It was as if I could only select one or the other. When I would visit a national park I was often quickly reminded of my love of nature and of why I needed to visit more frequently. If you are not yet aware of all of the amazing benefits I am sharing them here with you.

- **Silence & Sound:** Parks like Olympic and Isle Royale provide rare, gentle quiet, ideal for sensory awareness.
- **Presence & Perspective:** Grand Canyon and Acadia offer scale and timeless beauty that quietly shift inner focus.
- **Walking Meditation:** Parks with open spaces—like Great Sand Dunes or Canyonlands—invite embodied mindfulness.
- **Deep Immersion:** Remote places like Isle Royale or Glacier invite prolonged presence in nature's embrace.

When we move slowly, breathe deeply and listen fully, every park becomes more than scenery, it becomes a teacher of presence. These practices are doorways into the timeless conversations between body, spirit, and earth. Being mindful takes intention.

I have to be mindful of this with every conversation and know that multi-tasking was viewed as a skill but when in conversation we must be present.

Mindfulness Connection Circle to Life

Mindfulness is more than a practice — it's a way of *being* fully alive.
It's a gentle reminder that life isn't waiting for us somewhere in the future… it's happening right here, in this very breath, in this heartbeat, in this moment. You have read this throughout the book.

When we slow down and become present, we begin to see life's quiet beauty — the way light dances through a window, the sound of our own breath, the feeling of gratitude rising for no reason at all.
Mindfulness connects us back to what truly matters: our inner peace, our relationships, and the sacred rhythm of being human.

Each mindful breath is an act of self-love.
Each pause is an invitation to listen — not just to the world around us, but to the wisdom within us.
Through mindfulness, we learn that life isn't something to rush through; it's something to *experience*, to *feel*, and to *cherish*.

So as you move through this activity, allow yourself to soften into awareness.
Let your senses awaken.
Let your heart remember that mindfulness isn't separate from life — it *is* life, lived deeply, fully, and with love.

Mindfulness & It's connection to life

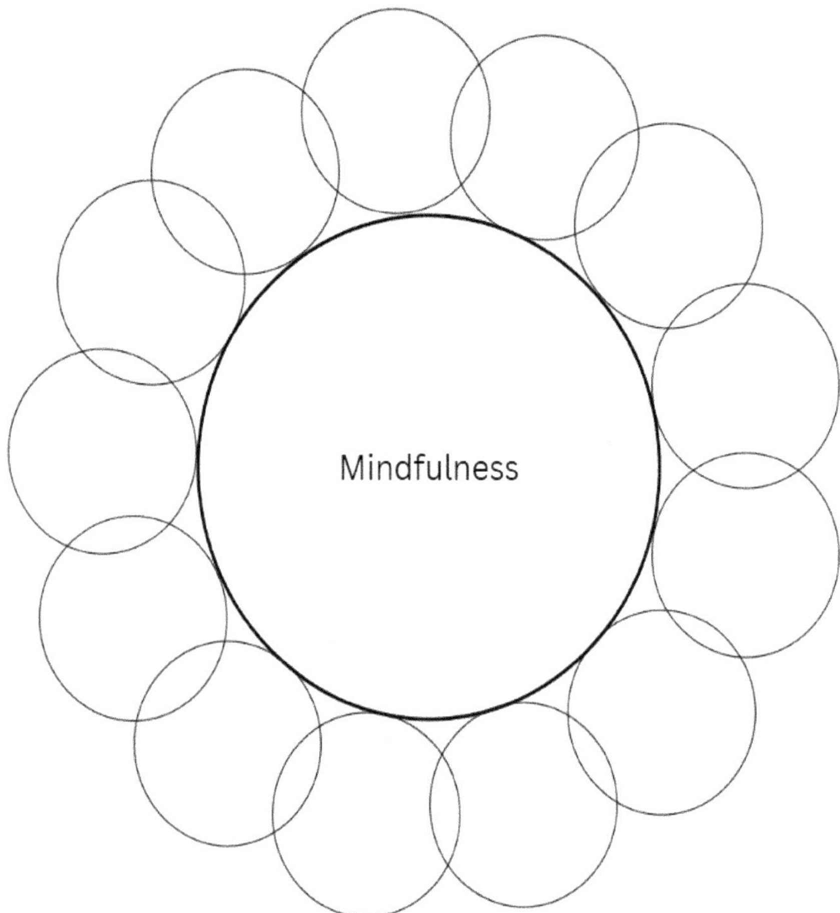

Fill in each of the circles for a visual on the areas that mindfulness are connected in your life and or where you would like to practice mindfulness frequently.

Add a bit of color by using different color ink pens

What 60 Seconds of Mindfulness Can Do

Imagine pausing for just one mindful minute each day:

- 🌿 **Stress melts** as your nervous system resets.
- 💭 **Mental clarity sharpens**, helping you focus better.
- 💓 **Heart rate slows**, inviting calm and balance.
- 🌸 **Emotions soften**, creating more patience and compassion.
- 🛑 **Overthinking pauses**, giving you a mental "reset button."
- 🌙 **Better sleep**, as your body learns to let go of tension.
- 🎨 **Creativity awakens**, because stillness makes room for new ideas.

Over time, these tiny pauses build up—like drops of water filling a well—until your life feels lighter, calmer, and more intentional.

"Each morning we are born again. What we do today matters most." ***-Buddah***

Everyday Mindfulness

100 Everyday Mindfulness Tips & Tools

Mindfulness doesn't have to mean sitting perfectly still on a cushion with your eyes closed, I mentioned this at the start of the book and now as I come to a close, I want to remind you. In fact, the real magic of mindfulness happens in the *everyday moments* — while you're cooking dinner, waiting in line, folding laundry, driving to work, or laughing with a friend.

I want to help you bring mindfulness into your *real life* — the life that sometimes feels busy, noisy, unpredictable, and full. That's why I created this section filled with simple, everyday ideas and tools you can add to your routine over the next three months (and beyond). Think of it as mindfulness on the go — practices you can carry with you wherever you are.

These ideas are meant to be flexible and fun — something you can share with your family, your children, your coworkers, or friends. You'll find that the more you practice, the more natural it becomes to slow down, breathe, notice, and respond with intention rather than reaction.

Everyday mindfulness isn't about doing something extra — it's about *doing what you already do* with more awareness and presence. Over time, these small, consistent moments of mindfulness can transform how you think, how you show up, and how you connect — with yourself and the world around you.

So, whether you have five minutes or fifty, I invite you to explore these practices with curiosity. Try one a day, or repeat your favorites. Share them, gift them, and let them ripple through your life and into the lives of others. Some of these were added throughout the book and are repeated here in this section.

Mindful Mornings

Oh, how easy it has become to pick up our cell phones first thing in the morning to check social media first thing. Starting the morning out with being intentional helps to make your day run so much smoother. Some cannot understand how I could forget my cell phone at home a couple times per month, LOL it was due to implementing this practice of not picking the phone up first thing in the morning unless it was with the purpose of texting someone. I have had times where I walk out the door and then feel like I am missing something important to discover "My cell phone is not with me" that feeling is a not so good one. Don't forget your cell phone. Try this in the mornings before picking it up.

1. Take three deep breaths before getting out of bed.

2. Set an intention for your day before checking your phone.

3. Listen to the morning sounds around you — birds, the hum of life starting up.

4. Make your first sip of water or tea a meditation in gratitude.

5. Open the blinds and take 30 seconds to really *see* the morning light.

6. Name one thing you're looking forward to today.

7. Stretch slowly and feel your body waking up.

8. Smile before your feet hit the floor — even if you don't feel like it.

9. Make brushing your teeth a mindfulness practice — feel the motion, taste the mint.

10. Notice your thoughts before they pull you into autopilot.

Mindful Movement

Being intentional about movement is something that I have to keep in mind. When we sit all day and are often busy we have to set timers and make sure we take breaks. Our family has this saying "If you don't use it, you lose it." move your body. I have found if I am not moving my body frequently enough, I get stiff and someone lazy and find myself gaining a few unnecessary pounds.

1. Go for a short walk without your phone.
2. Feel your feet connect with the ground — one step at a time.
3. Do one task — like washing dishes — with complete focus on movement and sound.
4. Try gentle stretching and breathe through each movement.
5. Notice your posture while sitting — how your body feels supported.
6. Take a slow, conscious breath between emails or tasks.
7. Do five slow shoulder rolls to release tension.
8. Drive without music for a few minutes, noticing the rhythm of motion.
9. Practice yoga or mindful dancing to release stored emotions.
10. Feel gratitude for your body and everything it allows you to experience.

Mindful Mindset

Our minds are powerful. Mindset matters more than most realize. It can make or break you. Be mindful of what you spend the majority of the time thinking about.

1. Practice noticing — not judging — your thoughts.
2. Pause before responding to stress; take one slow breath.
3. Remind yourself: "This moment is temporary."
4. Write down one limiting belief and replace it with truth.
5. Choose one word to guide your day (peace, clarity, flow, joy).
6. Accept that some days will feel messy — and that's okay.
7. When you feel overwhelmed, whisper, "I am here now."
8. Reframe mistakes as lessons — mindfulness in action.
9. Celebrate small wins.
10. Be kind to yourself as you would to a friend.

Mindful Moments at Work

1. Before a meeting, take one grounding breath.
2. Notice how your body feels after sitting for an hour — stretch gently.
3. Keep a small stone, crystal, or token on your desk to bring you back to the present.
4. Listen fully when someone speaks — no multitasking.
5. Step outside for 2 minutes between tasks.

6. Practice gratitude for your paycheck, your purpose, or your growth.

7. Use your breaks for breathing, not scrolling.

8. Write one sentence in a journal about what went well today.

9. Turn off notifications for 10 minutes and notice the peace.

10. End your day by mentally closing the "work tab" before going home.

Mindful Breathing & Grounding

1. Try the 4-7-8 breathing method (inhale 4, hold 7, exhale 8).
2. Place your hand on your heart and feel it beating.
3. Use the "5-4-3-2-1" grounding technique: notice 5 things you see, 4 you touch, 3 you hear, 2 you smell, 1 you taste.
4. Practice box breathing (inhale 4, hold 4, exhale 4, hold 4).
5. Breathe in peace, breathe out stress.
6. Notice your breath without trying to change it.
7. Feel your lungs expand — honor that you are alive.
8. Visualize roots growing from your feet deep into the earth.
9. Repeat a mantra with each breath (like "I am safe," "I am present").
10. Use scent (essential oils or candles) to anchor you to the now.

Mindful Relationships

1. When talking with someone, look them in the eyes and truly listen.

2. Give compliments mindfully — sincerely and thoughtfully.

3. Take a pause before reacting in anger.

4. Practice forgiveness for yourself and others.

5. Express gratitude out loud to loved ones.

6. Unplug during meals and focus on connection.

7. Hug someone for a full 10 seconds — feel the heartbeat.

8. Say “thank you” more often and mean it.

9. Set a mindful intention before difficult conversations.

10. Release the need to always be right — choose peace.

Mindful Technology Use

1. Schedule “no-screen” hours daily.

2. Move your phone out of reach when sleeping.

3. Turn off push notifications for social media.

4. Unfollow accounts that trigger comparison.

5. Mindfully select what you consume online.

6. Replace 10 minutes of scrolling with journaling.

7. When you pick up your phone, ask “Why?”
8. Create a digital vision board that inspires presence, not pressure.
9. Use a calming wallpaper that reminds you to breathe.
10. Try one tech-free day per week.

Mindful Self-Care

1. Journal your thoughts each night — release them onto paper.
2. Take a mindful shower, noticing the warmth and scent.
3. Eat slowly — chew, taste, enjoy.
4. Sip your coffee or tea without distractions.
5. Give yourself permission to rest.
6. Listen to frequency music, sound bowls, or soothing nature sounds.
7. Spend time outdoors every day, even briefly.
8. Thank your body for carrying you through the day.
9. Take a nap without guilt.
10. Light a candle and breathe in peace.
11. Use a calming wallpaper that reminds you to breathe.
12. Try one tech-free day per week.

Mindful Evenings

1. Reflect on one moment that made you smile today.

2. Do a short body scan before bed.

3. Put your phone away an hour before sleep.

4. Read something uplifting before bed.

5. Write down one thing you learned today.

6. Visualize releasing the day's worries.

7. Dim the lights and move slowly — prepare your body for rest.

8. Say three things you're grateful for before sleeping.

9. Forgive yourself for anything undone.

10. Fall asleep with peaceful music or guided meditation.

Mindful Living & Awareness

1. Practice gratitude while doing chores.
2. Notice the colors and textures around you.
3. Spend a few minutes in silence daily.
4. Smile at a stranger.
5. Practice patience in line or traffic.
6. Pause before spending money — ask if it aligns with your values.
7. Keep a "mindful moments" journal.
8. Celebrate your growth often — big or small.
9. Practice being curious instead of judgmental.
10. Remember: mindfulness isn't about perfection — it's about *presence*.

Here are a few ways to bring mindful moments into your relationship:

1. Listen without planning your response. Give your full attention — not to fix, but to understand.

2. Use touch as a grounding tool. Hold hands, hug longer, or rest your head on their shoulder and just breathe together.

3. Express appreciation out loud. Mindfully notice what you love about them — and say it.

4. Pause before reacting during conflict. Take one breath. Notice what you feel before you speak.

5. Create a tech-free moment together. Share a meal, take a walk, or talk before bed with no distractions.

6. Practice gratitude together. End the day by sharing one thing you're grateful for in each other.

7. Be curious. Even if you've known them for years, ask questions as if you're learning them again.

Mindful love isn't about perfection — it's about presence. It's the awareness that each moment you share is a chance to reconnect, reset, and renew your bond. The more you both practice being fully *here*, the more depth, peace, and joy you'll find in your relationship.

Mindful Moments as a Parent

Parenting offers endless opportunities to practice mindfulness — sometimes by choice, and other times out of pure necessity. Between the noise, the schedules, the emotions (theirs and yours), it's easy to slip into autopilot. But mindfulness invites us to *pause*, breathe, and reconnect with the heart of what matters most — the moments we share with our children.

Being a mindful parent doesn't mean being perfect or calm all the time. It means being *aware* — of your emotions, your tone, your energy, and your presence. It's about showing up, not as a flawless version of yourself, but as a fully human one. When you practice mindfulness as a parent, you model it for your children — showing them how to be present, kind, and aware in their own lives. What families may realize is that there is a call for a more mindful, emotionally attuned approach. The world is faster, louder, more digital and more uncertain.

Children feel that energy just as adults do, Mindful parenting offers a grounding path forward. Emotional regulation is now a core parenting skill. With rising stress, digital overstimulation, parents who practice mindfulness are better equipped to model. Regardless of if you are a parent, teacher, aunt, grand-parent you can apply mindful skills to help you with calm responses, healthy boundaries, emotional vocabulary, and stress recovery as your regulated nervous system becomes a child's sense of safety. It took me some time to realize presence matters more than perfection. Having energy awareness helps to protect the home envrionement. Conscious communication is everything in this era. One of the phrases I find myself saying is “give me a moment to think about it” I raised my voice to let my kids know that I meant business. A mother of all boys, I was aware that I could not be the pretend, fake TV mom. In the real world with all boys, you will raise your voice to get their attention when they are horse playing around at inappropriate times. Our children become aware of our various facial expressions and they understand how far they can go. Implement mindfulness practices and add your own flavor to it. Time outs did not work with my sons, I tried this for about a year and a half, maybe two years on and off. It did not really make a huge impact for my sons. I needed to find another way to help them to understand they had a responsibility as well, to behave in public, to respect each other at home, to care about the presence of our home, we had chores, rules that they needed to respect and they understood what was considered as "embarrassing behaviors" I did as well, I knew yelling in the middle of the store would create an embarrassing moment for myself and my sons. Yelling in the car, " Stop it now" or "Put your seat belt back on now" was not embarrassing and had a tone of I mean business. As I look back on those were mindful moments. You can say yelling is really raising your tone to get the attention. THis obvious is not something one would do at work. If you are a mom, aunt, grammie, father, uncle, god-parent, I am sure you understand what I am stating here.

10 Everyday Mindfulness Moments for Parents

1. Pause before reacting. When your child pushes your buttons, take one deep breath before responding.

2. Listen with your full attention. When they talk, really *hear* them — not just their words, but their feelings.

3. Use morning routines as connection time. Instead of rushing, make eye contact, smile, or share a few words of gratitude together.

4. Create a "tech-free" zone. Even 15 minutes of undistracted play or conversation can strengthen connection.

5. Notice the small things. The way they laugh, how their hair falls across their face — these are fleeting moments.

6. Take mindful family walks. Listen to the sounds of nature together and talk about what you see or feel.

7. Practice mindful transitions. Before moving from one activity to another (like work to dinner), take a breath together to reset.

8. Model emotional awareness. When you're frustrated, say, "I'm feeling overwhelmed right now, so I'm going to take a few breaths."

9. End the day with gratitude. Share one thing you each appreciated about your day or each other.

10. Give yourself grace. When you fall short (and you will), be kind to yourself. That too is mindfulness in action.

Being present, emotionally regulated, aware of your energy, conscious of technology's impact, and willing to model the inner peace you want your child to experience. When we as parents strengthen our inner world, we help our kids to strengthen theirs. We blink our eyes and they are adults.

Mindful Parenting for Young Adult Children

The ability to shift from authority to ally. Your young adult may be legally grown, but emotionally, socially, and financially, this generation is navigating an incredibly complex world — and they need a different kind of support. Shifting from directing to guiding is important. My sons craved independence but still needed and continue to need mentorship. Mindful parenting recognizes the tension between:

- wanting to protect them
- needing to let them learn through experience

I have had to sit and think about ways I can help to support them without trying to be controlling. An area that I am working on is trying to ask before advising them as they at times appear defensive and may not share as much with me. Attempting to determine if they need advice, space or for me to simply listen is something I now ask. It appears to reduce conflict and helps to create a safe space for them to openly share.

Being perfect is not the goal but really working on my emotional reactions is an area I often have to think of and sometimes I fail.

Young adults face the following:

- identity shifts
- digital comparison
- economic pressure
- loneliness
- career uncertainty
- relationship complexities

They don't need judgment — they need grounding, empathy, and someone who sees them without filters.

Let Go of Old Parenting Scripts

Your role is no longer to correct or control.
Mindful parenting means replacing old patterns like:

- Lecturing
- Overexplaining
- assuming you know best
- Rescuing
- guilt-driven communication

Instead, shift into:

- Validating
- Listening
- co-creating solutions
- respecting their journey

You're no longer managing their life — you're helping them manage their *mindset*. Guide them into their own inner awareness rather than solving things for them. This builds confidence, not dependence. Mindfulness teaches parents of young adults to release emotional attachment to *how things "should" be*. When you're grounded, they feel safer coming home — literally or emotionally. This is the stage where relationships between parents and children can become deeply fulfilling — if both sides feel respected and understood. They did not explain it like this when we were kids, Mindfulness matters. The good news is, now we know. To know better is to do better.

The EyeThat Sees Within

Third Eye Chakra

As I came to the end of writing this book, I wanted to revisit— the **Third Eye Chakra.** It would feel incomplete to explore mindfulness without providing additional information for those who may not be aware of "What are Chakras" I have spoken with plenty of people who classify this as "woo woo stuff" I am not here to change your mind but to add valuable information that can assist you with tools and information to help you to you to get to know who you truly are outside of your name, birthdate, weight, height, being open to learning more about the essence of the true self requires us to have an open mind and to understand our bodies, minds and souls.

What Are Chakras?

Chakras are the body's **energy centers** — spinning wheels of energy that influence how we feel, think, and connect to ourselves and the world.
Each chakra relates to different aspects of our physical, emotional, and spiritual wellbeing, from feeling grounded and safe to expressing love, truth, and intuition.

When your chakras are balanced, energy flows freely and you feel centered, calm, and aligned.
When they're blocked or overactive, you might feel off balance — emotionally, mentally, or physically.

Mindfulness, breathwork, meditation, and sound healing can help bring these energy centers back into harmony. I know I explained a few things as it pertains to this chakra in the book already but, I am also adding the information here for you.

The Third Eye, known in Sanskrit as *Ajna*, is often described as the seat of intuition — the place where insight, perception, and wisdom awaken. But beyond the mystical descriptions, the Third Eye is where **mindfulness lives**. It is the space within us that observes without judgment, notices without reacting, and sees beyond the surface of things.

When we practice mindfulness, we are not just training the mind — we are awakening the Third Eye. We are strengthening our ability to see clearly: to witness our thoughts, to sense our emotions, and to understand life from a deeper, more centered place.

This chakra reminds us that **true sight isn't about what we see with our eyes open, but what we perceive when we close them.**
It's about trusting our inner knowing — that quiet wisdom that whispers truth when the world feels loud.

Mindfulness and the Third Eye are intertwined in the most profound way:

- Mindfulness clears the mental clutter so the Third Eye can open.
- The Third Eye, in turn, deepens mindfulness by allowing us to view life from a higher perspective.

> When awareness meets intuition, we begin to see life as it truly is — sacred, connected, and full of possibility.

In each of the books I make the connection to the chakra associated with the book, this book is complete, now that I have added this section honoring the energy center that ties it all together.

Because mindfulness isn't only about calming the mind — it's about *seeing with the soul.*

The Third Eye Chakra (Ajna)

Color: Indigo
Element: Light
Focus: Intuition, clarity, inner wisdom, spiritual insight

When your third eye is balanced, you trust your inner guidance, see truth beyond illusion, and move through life with clarity and awareness.

Third Eye Affirmations

1. *I trust my inner vision and allow my intuition to guide me.*
2. *I see clearly with both my physical and spiritual eyes.*
3. *My mind is calm, open, and receptive to divine wisdom.*

You can repeat these during meditation, journaling, or while looking softly into your own reflection.

Third Eye Meditation: "Awakening Inner Vision"

1. **Find stillness.** Sit comfortably with your spine tall. Close your eyes and take three deep, cleansing breaths — in through the nose, out through the mouth.
2. **Bring awareness to your third eye.** Focus gently on the space between your eyebrows — your inner point of vision.

3. **Visualize indigo light.** See a soft indigo glow forming there, radiating outward with each inhale.

4. **Breathe into clarity.** With each exhale, release mental fog, overthinking, or doubt.

5. **Affirm silently:** “I see clearly. I trust my intuition.”

6. **Sit in the stillness.** Allow any images, sensations, or insights to surface without judgment.

7. **Close with gratitude.** Thank your inner wisdom for always being available when you pause and listen.

(You can enhance this meditation with frankincense, sandalwood, or lavender essential oils — all of which support the Third Eye Chakra.)

Journal Prompt 

“What does my intuition feel like when it speaks to me — and how can I honor it more in my daily life?”

Encourage participants to describe how intuition shows up for them

(through feelings, sensations, dreams, or knowing), and reflect on moments they followed — or ignored — that guidance.

Mindful Exercise: “Intuitive Noticing”

This simple yet powerful activity strengthens third-eye awareness through mindful observation.

1. Step outside or sit quietly near a window.

2. Take a few slow breaths, and choose one object or detail to focus on — a leaf, a shadow, a pattern, or a sound.

3. Observe without labeling or judging. Notice the colors, textures, and feelings it stirs within you.

4. Ask inwardly: *What does this moment want to show me?*

5. Write or reflect on any insights or sensations that arise — sometimes intuition speaks in whispers through everyday awareness.

I was inspired for so many reasons to write this book series as I became more and more aware of the importance of our mental wellbeing as a society. In my first book, "Journaling is good for our mental health" I share with you how I came into Journaling, book two "Say It like you Mean It Affirmations Really Do Work" I share how mindset plays an important role in our lives, the way we think and how we speak.

Realizing many of the struggles that I had faced at some point in my life were struggles for others as well but they were lacking the tools. Failures of wellbeing happen when we forget or do not know how to take care of ourselves. In actuality it really is not a failure but more of a gentle wake up call. The moments when we drift away from our center, forget our needs, or stop listening to what our body, mind, and spirit are trying to tell us. Going against all that your mind and body is speaking to you eventually creates unhappiness. From a practical view, a failure of wellbeing is simply a **misalignment** — when your actions no longer match what your inner self truly needs. Mental awareness is necessary to help keep you healthy.

Connection is power in mindfulness, do not forget this. When connection fades — whether it's connection to ourselves, our purpose, or to others — suffering often grows.

Purpose guides you toward the *next* — it gives meaning to the choices you make in each mindful moment.

Mindfulness asks,

> "What am I experiencing right now?"

Purpose asks,

> "Why does this moment matter?"

When you live with both questions asked at once, your everyday actions — how you speak, eat, love, and lead — become expressions of your deeper truth. Together, they create alignment between your thoughts, actions, and values. Mindfulness helps you hear the quiet whisper of your purpose — and purpose gives mindfulness direction.Together, they invite you to live not just *in the moment*, but *from the heart*.

Lastly, I mentioned the third eye chakra, which is also about Insight. Insight turns mindfulness from a calming technique into a tool for **transformation**.

It helps you: recognize unhealthy patterns or limiting beliefs.

- Understand what truly nourishes your peace and purpose.
- Respond with wisdom rather than react from habit.
- Develop self-compassion through understanding rather than judgment.

Through mindfulness, we learn to observe. Through insight, we learn to *see clearly* — and that clarity sets us free. At the start of this book, I dedicated the book to a specific group of people and as the book now comes to a close, I am also dedicating this book to the skeptic, the one who says "I don't believe in all of that stuff" yet you find yourself often unhappy, unfulfilled, and surrounded by powerful negatives. I am extending an invitation to you to check out other books in my Jamm With Me A Journey To Your Higher Self, series. It is my hope that you "get the point" and can find a handful of tools shared to help you to get to know who you truly are and to live authentically.

I often speak about resilience and want to add that this is not something that happens overnight. I want to share an activity that I learned when obtaining a mindfulness certification. True resilience acknowledges the difficulty of the situation and choosing to move forward and not allowing that situation to cripple you permanently. Stay in reality, be aware, observe and always return to "Breath" mindfulness is a powerful tool that helps us to reconnect with the present.

A space where you can pause, breath and simply be. Paying attention on purpose to the present moment is a skill. Mindfulness is a teacher, it is an act of centering ourselves and allows us to respond from a place of calm and mental awareness. Mindfulness will help you to make better decisions. A tool that reminds us we are not defined by our past. Embrace the power, it is not a destination or a goal to achieve, it is you meeting you where you are. Get to know you. I have provided a solid foundation for you to take your mindfulness practice to the next level. When practicing mindfulness you will notice that it is not a fairy tale or woo woo thing where you only feel positive emotions all the time or are one hundred percent focused all the time. Mindfulness, like any meaningful skill, isn't something we master overnight — it's something we *grow into* through repetition, patience, and commitment. Never forget this.

Think about it:

- A **swimmer** doesn't glide through the water gracefully the first time they dive in — they train their body to find rhythm and endurance.

- A **basketball player** doesn't sink three-pointers by accident — they practice their form, focus, and timing over and over again.

- A **runner** doesn't win races simply by wanting to — they strengthen their muscles and mindset through consistent training.

- A **public speaker** doesn't step on stage with confidence without rehearsal — they practice their message until it flows naturally.

- A **musician** doesn't create harmony from chaos without patience — they tune, adjust, and return to their instrument daily.

- A **chef** doesn't craft a perfect dish on the first try — they refine flavors, textures, and timing through repetition.

- Even a **gardener** must nurture their plants — watering, pruning, and waiting — trusting the unseen growth beneath the soil.

- And just as an **author** writes, rewrites, and edits before their story fully takes shape, mindfulness too unfolds through continual practice and reflection.

Mindfulness works the same way. You can't rush inner calm, awareness, or emotional balance any more than you can rush a seed to bloom.
Each time you pause to breathe, observe your thoughts, or return to the present moment, you're strengthening your "mindfulness muscle."

Some days it will feel effortless — other days it may feel like work. But every moment of practice matters, because mindfulness isn't about perfection; it's about presence.

Over time, those small moments of awareness become your new rhythm — just as the swimmer finds their stroke, the musician finds their sound, and the runner finds their pace. Mindfulness is a practice — not a performance. The more you show up for it, the more it shows up for you.

Use the below photo of the anchor as a part of an activity. Get in a comfortable position sitting up.

1) Place your finger under your nose and feel your breath going in and out. Can you feel it?
2) Place your hand on your chest, over your heart. Can you feel your hand moving when you breathe?
3) Place your hand on your belly and feel the movement of your breathing there.
4) Put your hands on your needs and breathe naturally. Notice where you feel movement of your breath most easily. Is it just beneath your nose, at your chest or at your belly?
5) Now, rest your attention on your anchor and see if you can keep your body relaxed at the same time. This is how we rest in the feeling of the movement of our breath

Allow the anchor to be a reminder of grounding, returning to home and to use your breath to help you get there.

After completing this book, I felt called to add one more reflection — one that touches the tender space of loss.

Recently, my family experienced a loss that reminded me how essential mindfulness is during times of grief, endings, and transition.

The next section is dedicated to anyone navigating change, heartbreak, or loss — may these words bring you stillness, compassion, and peace.

Grief is not linear, and it has no timetable.

Some days may feel lighter, while others may catch you off guard. A scent, a song, a place, or even a quiet moment can suddenly remind you of the person you miss. This doesn't mean you are moving backward — it means your love was deep, and your connection was real.

Mindfulness gives us the space to breathe through these waves instead of fighting them. It invites us to honor our emotions, to sit gently with our memories, and to recognize that healing doesn't require forgetting.

It also reminds us to fully embrace those who remain — the loved ones still here, the relationships that comfort us, and the moments that continue to hold beauty despite our pain.

May you cherish the memories of those who have transitioned while staying present enough to experience the love, support, and life that still surrounds you.

Mindfulness in Times of Loss

When Life Changes: Practicing Mindfulness Through Loss

Loss — whether through death, heartbreak, or life transition — shakes our sense of stability. It can feel like the ground beneath us has shifted, leaving us unsure of who we are or what comes next.

Mindfulness doesn't erase that pain — it *creates space* for it.
It allows us to sit with what is, instead of rushing to fix, deny, or escape it.

Mindfulness invites us to meet our grief, confusion, and sadness with gentle awareness. It teaches us that healing doesn't come from avoiding discomfort but from being present with it — breath by breath, moment by moment.

How to Implement Mindfulness During Loss

1. Pause and Breathe

When emotions surge — sadness, anger, guilt, or fear — pause.
Take one conscious breath.
Notice how the body feels.
You don't need to change the emotion; simply *name* it: "This is grief," or "This is uncertainty."
Naming your emotion helps anchor you in awareness rather than being swept away by it.

2. Allow, Don't Resist

Mindfulness is about *allowing* what is present.
Grief unfolds in waves — sometimes calm, sometimes overwhelming.
Instead of pushing it away, give yourself permission to feel it fully,

knowing it's part of being human.
Whisper to yourself: "It's okay to feel this. It's safe to be here now." My husband and I have both had loved ones to transition. This section is dedicated to both our families and for you, your loved ones and friends that may have experienced someone passing on to the other side, returning to the non-physical form.

3. Stay Present with the Body

Loss often pulls us into the past or the "what ifs" of the future.
Grounding into the body can bring us back.
Notice your breath.
Feel your feet on the floor.
Place a hand over your heart and sense your own warmth — a reminder that you're still here, still living, still breathing.

4. Be Kind to Yourself

Mindfulness without compassion becomes cold observation.
So practice *kind awareness*.
When you catch your inner voice saying, "I should be over this," or "I can't handle this," gently replace it with:

> "I'm doing the best I can right now."

Self-compassion is mindfulness in motion.

5. Observe Change Without Judgment

Loss reminds us that all things change — people, jobs, roles, relationships, even identities.
Mindfulness helps us witness that change instead of resisting it.
By observing impermanence, we begin to see that while circumstances shift, our capacity to heal and find meaning remains constant.

A Mindful Reminder 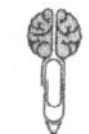

You can't rush healing — but you can walk through it consciously. You can breathe through the ache, feel without drowning, and learn to trust that each moment of presence is an act of healing itself.

> "Even in loss, the breath continues.
> Each inhale reminds us we are still connected to life."

Journal Prompt

"What am I learning about myself through this loss?"

"Where can I soften and show myself more compassion right now?"

Four Week Mindful Affirmation Challenge

I love offering you a variety of tools, challenges, and options because growth isn't one-size-fits-all — and your mindfulness practice deserves support from every angle. This 4-week Affirmation Challenge is one more way to help you keep moving forward with intention.

These affirmations can be written on sticky notes and placed anywhere you'll see them — on your mirror, inside your car, or right on your desk. Small reminders create big shifts. Be prepared to do your thing and do it well.

Here's the truth:
We often tell ourselves, *"Nah, that's too much,"* or *"I don't need to do all that."* But living your best life requires mindful effort. Not perfection. Not pressure. So many people want to be happy and have the best possible life but become too comfortable with putting in little effort. Stop talking yourself out of growth, self discovery and walking the path for your journey. As a child I was often inspired by people of all ages who were motivated, had goals and were not afraid to show up. I also enjoyed watching tv series and as I am writing this, one show comes to mind.

I recall the introduction to a TV series, Fame, "*You've got big dreams, dreams cost and right here is where you start paying in sweat*" Let's rephrase this; "You've got big dreams. You want a peaceful, aligned, elevated life.

Well, growth has a cost —and the first place you invest is within yourself."

"This is where you begin...with intention, with patience, with your daily practice."

Effort. Consistency. Presence is necessary.

Our evolution happens when we're willing to show up, even in little ways. When we place the reminder on the mirror. When we pause. When we choose a thought that supports who we're becoming.

Your journey to the best version of yourself begins with these small, intentional moments — and this challenge is designed to meet you right where you are while helping you leap forward.

Week 1: Awareness — "Seeing Yourself Clearly"

Theme: Slowing down, noticing thoughts, tuning into inner truth.
Goal: Build presence and conscious self-observation.

Daily Affirmations

Day 1: *I pause. I notice. I am here.*
Day 2: *My thoughts are not facts; I choose what I follow.*
Day 3: *I honor what my body is telling me.*
Day 4: *I am becoming more aware of what nurtures me.*
Day 5: *I allow clarity to rise naturally.*
Day 6: *I see myself with honesty and compassion.*
Day 7: *Every moment is a new opportunity to reconnect.*

Mindful Practice of the Week

5-minute "Notice What's Here" check-in:

- What am I thinking?
- What am I feeling emotionally?

- What is my body trying to tell me?
- What do I need?

Week 2: Acceptance — "Allowing What Is"

Theme: Releasing resistance, softening judgment, embracing emotions.
Goal: Practice being with your inner world without trying to fix it.

Daily Affirmations

Day 1: *I accept myself in this moment as I am.*
Day 2: *It's okay for me to feel what I feel.*
Day 3: *I release the need to prove anything to anyone.*
Day 4: *I give myself permission to rest and reset.*
Day 5: *My emotions have wisdom; I listen without fear.*
Day 6: *Acceptance brings me peace and inner freedom.*
Day 7: *I am worthy of compassion — especially from myself.*

Mindful Practice of the Week

The "Softening Breath": Inhale for 4, exhale for 6.
Repeat 10 times while gently saying internally: *"Let it be."*

Week 3: Alignment — "Returning to Your Truth"

Theme: Clarifying values, aligning energy, tuning into inner direction.
Goal: Move from automatic living to intentional living.

Daily Affirmations

Day 1: *I move in the direction of what feels true for me.*
Day 2: *I honor my boundaries with ease and confidence.*
Day 3: *I choose thoughts that support my emotional well-being.*
Day 4: *My energy is sacred; I manage it with intention.*
Day 5: *I align my actions with my highest values.*
Day 6: *It is safe for me to grow and evolve.*
Day 7: *I trust my inner guidance fully.*

Mindful Practice of the Week

"Energy Audit" journal prompt:

- What drains me?
- What nourishes me?
- What can I release?
- What deserves more of my attention?

Week 4: Action — "Mindful Momentum"

Theme: Gentle forward movement, intentional choices, embodied mindfulness.
Goal: Live the affirmations rather than simply recite them.

Daily Affirmations

Day 1: *Today I take one small step that supports my future self.*
Day 2: *I move with purpose, not pressure.*
Day 3: *I act from alignment, not fear or comparison.*
Day 4: *My actions reflect the love I have for myself.*
Day 5: *I create space for joy, peace, and possibility.*
Day 6: *I trust the timing of my life.*
Day 7: *I am becoming the version of me I was always meant to be.*

A Journey to Your Higher Self

Every book in this series has been a stepping stone — a guided elevation — designed to help you rise into the version of yourself that is wiser, more grounded, more aligned, and more powerful.

Book One, Two & Three were about awakened awareness and our mental health through Journaling, nurtured healing, the power of the mind and emotional expansion through affirmations, as well as strengthened your mindset, your energy, and your inner resilience through meditation. Revisiting our belief systems, relearning truths and so much more.

Together, they prepared you for the next phase of your evolution: **Book Four — the embodiment of your Higher Self through mindfulness.**

Because becoming your higher self is not an event or a destination. It is a practice. A daily unfolding. A continuous remembering of who you truly are beneath layers of stress, fear, ego, or conditioning. And mindfulness is the key that unlocks this remembering.

We have been conditioned most of our life to believe there is only one way but, I am here to share with you a variety of ways to help you in this life's journey to becoming your happiest, healthiest and in harmony with yourself. "Self connection" which leads to an overall better connection with those in your life through mindfulness.

Not everyone is meant to remain in our lives forever. There may be a season that comes where change happens, be mindful of what these relationships taught you. We are often learning and growing even when through tough times, you have learned that mindfulness is still a presence.

How Mindfulness Supports the Journey to Your Higher Self

One of the most liberating truths mindfulness teaches us is this:

Not everyone will like you — and that is perfectly okay. Mindfulness invites you to look inward rather than attach your worth to external approval. As you grow, evolve, and step into your purpose, you may notice that some people become uncomfortable. This discomfort isn't actually about you — it's about what your success, confidence, or self-awareness reflects back to them. Most people spend years trying to fit in, be accepted, or avoid conflict. But mindfulness teaches you to ask:

> *Who am I trying to impress? Who am I shrinking for? Is this authentic to me?* When you operate from your inner truth, you naturally stop bending yourself to please others. Your personal evolution may highlight someone else's stagnation.

Your confidence may reveal their insecurity. Your consistency may expose their excuses. Your success may remind them of dreams they abandoned. When people don't yet understand their own inner world, they can project outward stories such as:

"She thinks she's better than everyone."
"He's changed."
"They act differently now."

Mindfulness helps you see these reactions clearly — without internalizing them. Instead of taking things personally, mindfulness allows you to pause and recognize:

"This is their perception, not my identity." I like to say, "not mine yours or not mine theirs" You can acknowledge their discomfort without carrying it. You can stay grounded without explaining yourself.

You can remain kind without shrinking your light. This skill protects your peace, especially when your growth triggers emotional reactions in others. When you're authentic, you won't align with every person, circle, workplace, or community — and that's a sign you're growing into who you're meant to be. Fitting in is external. Belonging is internal.

And mindfulness guides you back to belonging to **yourself**.

Instead of thinking: **"They don't like me."** Shift toward:

"I am no longer shrinking myself to make others comfortable."

"I am honoring my growth, even when it changes relationships."

"Not everyone is meant to walk every chapter of my life with me, and that's okay."

Mindfulness is more than presence — it's awareness with intention. It is the ability to observe your inner world with clarity instead of judgment, and to choose response over reaction. This is exactly what the higher self does. When you practice mindfulness, you begin to:

1. Hear Your Inner Guidance Clearly

The higher self speaks in intuition, nudges, and inner knowing. Mindfulness quiets the mental noise so you can hear the truth beneath it.

2. Release Old Identities and Patterns

Becoming your higher self requires letting go of habits, beliefs, or wounds that no longer support your growth.

Mindfulness helps you notice these patterns as they arise — giving you the power to choose differently.

3. Strengthen Emotional Intelligence

Your higher self responds with wisdom, not impulsiveness. Mindfulness teaches you to sit with emotions, understand them, and move through them consciously.

4. Create Alignment in Thoughts, Actions, and Energy

When you are present, you make choices that match your values and your vision.
This alignment is where your higher self lives.

5. Cultivate Compassion — for Yourself and Others

Your higher self is rooted in love, not fear.
Mindfulness softens the self-judgment and strengthens empathy, making it easier to lead, communicate, and show up from a place of love.

Mindfulness as Embodiment, Not Just Awareness

To embody your higher self means you don't just *know* who you are becoming — you begin to *live* it:

- You breathe with intention.
- You communicate with presence.
- You calm your nervous system instead of operating in survival mode.
- You choose peace, clarity, and emotional balance.
- You show up aligned with your purpose rather than your patterns.

Mindfulness transforms the higher self from a concept into a lived reality.

It shifts you from **becoming** your higher self to actually **being** your higher self.

Stepping Fully Into Your Higher Self

You have reached the end of this book, but not the end of your journey. In fact, this is where the real transformation begins — not in the reading, but in the living.

Throughout this series, you have been guided layer by layer into deeper awareness of who you are, what you carry, and what you are capable of becoming.

Each book has lifted you to a new level, preparing you for the next elevation:

- Awareness
- Healing
- Growth
- Embodiment

Now, with the lessons in this book, you have entered the space where mindfulness becomes your daily companion. It becomes the quiet strength behind your decisions, the grounding anchor in your challenges, and the gentle reminder of the higher self that has always been within you.

Mindfulness teaches you to return home to yourself — to notice, to breathe, to respond with intention rather than react from fear or old patterns.

It gives you the clarity to hear your inner wisdom, the courage to release what no longer serves you, and the presence to choose the path that aligns with your highest truth. Your higher self is no longer a distant concept. It is the part of yourself you are learning to embody every day.

When you choose stillness over chaos, compassion over criticism, awareness over autopilot, you honor your evolution. You are not striving to become someone new — you are remembering who you've always been.

This book, and the series as a whole, has simply lit the path. But *you* are the one walking it. You are the one doing the work. You are the one expanding, aligning, and rising.

So as you close these pages, carry this truth with you:

You are ready.
You are capable.
You are powerful.
And you are already becoming your higher self.

Continue to practice mindfulness. Continue to choose presence. Continue to trust your journey.

Your evolution is a lifelong unfolding — and this is just the beginning of your next beautiful chapter.

A Letter To You

Dear Beautiful Soul,

Congratulations! This book is lengthy but filled with amazing mindfulness tips, tools, reminders and one that you can revisit parts of often. Take a moment to thank yourself for reading the book, for pausing and being present. Gratitude helps to anchor the experience. Ask yourself "what did I become aware of?" Set an intention going forward as you are ending your reading here to carry what you have learned about mindfulness with you in your day to day life. Make it a practice and help others. Please remember that peace is always within reach and that you can return here anytime by being mindful.

Mindfulness is a lifelong practice and not a destination but a way of being. It's something we return to again and again, not to become perfect, but to become present. We have to have the courage to remove distractions by putting our phone on silent or airplane mode, turn off the TV or step away from noisy places if possible. As you close this book, consider choosing just one practice, a mindful breath, a gratitude pause, or a moment of stillness each day. Let that be your doorway back to the now. May you continue to walk gently, breathe deeply and live fully in each moment. Practice is always waiting for you, right here, right now.

In conclusion, here are a few quotes of Jon Kabat-Zinn, the founder of the Center of Mindfulness at University of Massachusetts Medical School that could inspire you.

"Mindfulness is a way of befriending ourselves and our experience."

"The best way to capture moments is to pay attention. This is how we cultivate mindfulness."

"Mindfulness means being awake. It means knowing what you are doing"

As you turn the final page, know this:

The power of mindfulness already lives within you. It's in your breath, your body, your awareness. Every pause is a beginning. Every breath is an invitation. You do not need a perfect setting or a long period of stretch time, you will only need to be willing and present. Whether you are doing laundry, cooking dinner, walking or listening to a family member or a friend, your life itself is the practice. Please keep coming back to this moment time and time again. It is enough. And, know that **You are enough**.

Stay tuned for book five in the Jamm with me A Journey to your higher self book series, Spirituality A New Understanding

Sincerely, Shanta

Sati-sampajanna. It means mindfulness and clear comprehension.

JAMM WITH ME A JOURNEY TO YOUR HIGHER SELF book titles

Pick Up A Pen Journaling Is Good for Our Mental Health

Say It Like You Mean It Affirmation Really Do Work

A Bridge To Finding Peace Within

They Didn't Explain It Like This When We Were Kids

Book five pending release, which is the last book in this five part series. **A New Understanding Of Spiritual**

Below are the Journal Books, an Adult coloring book line as well as a children's journal and coloring book line, Released By Shanta Generally, which are all available for purchase on Amazon or at **www.authenticyoumindset.com**

Self Care Journal, not pictured

References:

https://positivepsychology.com/mindfulness-therapy

www.authentictalks2.com

https://www.harvard.edu/in-focus/mindfulness-meditation

https://gradschool.princeton.edu/events/2025/building-resilience-mindfulness-and-stress-management-academic-professional-success

https://mindfulmusehealing.com

https://www.uclahealth.org/uclamindful

https://www.uclahealth.org/programs/uclamindful/facilitating-mindfulness

Mindfulness Meditation for Resilience | Casandra Brene Brown Motivational Speech

https://www.massachusetts.edu

https://cambridgeinsight.org/the-wisdom-of-embodied-mindfulness/

https://www.mayoclinic.org/healthy-lifestyle/consumer-health/in-depth/mindfulness-exercises/art-20046356

https://www.mindful.org/what-is-mindfulness/

https://www.mindful.org/join-the-mindful-affirmations-4-week-challenge/

www.ingramcontent.com/pod-product-compliance
Lightning Source LLC
LaVergne TN
LVHW050614100826
845148LV00011B/1587

* 9 7 9 8 9 8 5 4 4 3 6 4 6 *